GREAT PIES
YOU CAN BAKE

LOIS HILL

Illustrated by Clair Moritz

GRAMERCY BOOKS
New York • Avenel, New Jersey

No man's pie is freed from his ambitious finger
—Shakespeare, Henry VIII

This 1992 edition is published by Gramercy Books,
distributed by Outlet Book Company, Inc., a Random
House Company, 40 Engelhard Avenue, Avenel,
New Jersey 07001.

Printed and bound in the United States of America

Library of Congress Cataloging-in-Publication Data

Hill, Lois.
    Great pies you can bake / Lois Hill.
        p.   cm.
    Includes index.
    ISBN 0-517-05157-5
    1. Pies   I. Title.   II. Title: Great pies you
can bake.
TX773.H519   1991
641.8'652—dc20   90-43741
                                                    CIP

10   9   8   7   6   5   4   3   2

Contents

ACKNOWLEDGMENTS

Grateful acknowledgment for recipes and advice is offered to
Glorya Hale, Susan Liebegott, Sharon Mazer, Jamila Miller,
Clair Moritz, Jennifer Moyer, Phyllis Sternau, and Susan Sternau.

Introduction

Chuse your materials right;
From them of course the figure will arise,
And elegance adorn the surface of your pies.

—Kingsley

PIE. n.s. [This word is derived by *Skinner* from *biezan* to build, that is, to build of paste; by *Junius* derived by contraction from *pasty;* if pasties, doubled together without walls, were the first pies, the derivation is easy from *pie* a foot; as in some provinces, an apple pasty is still called an apple foot.]
1. Any crust baked with something in it.

—Samuel Johnson
A Dictionary of the English Language (1837)

For everyone who bakes pies or anyone who has ever dreamed of making a pie, *Great Pies You Can Bake* offers a compendium of pies for all occasions, tastes, and seasons. There are apple pies; other fruit pies, including citrus pies; cream, custard, and chiffon pies; pumpkin pies; ice cream pies; special pies; tarts; sugar-free pies; an assortment of savory pies and quiches; and numerous kinds of crusts. Recipes are arranged by category, and are alphabetical within each section, except where a variation follows a master recipe.

Save room for the pie! Whether it's part of the main course or a special dessert, an attractive, delicious pie is always the centerpiece of a meal. Here are tips and suggestions for successful pie baking:

- Assemble all ingredients before you begin.
- Always preheat the oven for at least 15 minutes before baking, or until the oven thermometer indicates that the desired temperature has been reached. Know the quirks of your oven. Baking times listed in recipes are based on standard oven temperatures. If your oven runs hot, check frequently for browning; if it is slow, allow for extra baking time.
- Use standard measuring utensils. Accurate measurements are essential for successful pie dough.
- Equipment: Ovenproof glass, ceramic, or blackened metal pie pans are better than lightweight aluminum. Two knives may be substituted for a pastry blender or food processor (see below), but they make much more work for the cook. A good ball-bearing-type rolling pin will last a lifetime, but a wine bottle with the label soaked off is a handy substitute for an impromptu pie. Wire cooling racks help to cool pies quickly.
- A food processor fitted with a pastry or dough blade may be used in place of a pastry blender—and takes the hard work out of making a crust. Briefly process the flour and shortening, then add the water, as if working by hand.

- Always use fresh, all-purpose flour for pie crusts. Flour picks up moisture as it ages; old flour changes the chemistry of the pie dough—for the worse.
- To catch any drips or spills, place a baking sheet on the oven rack beneath the pie.
- The first rule of successful pie dough is that the less it is handled, the more tender it will be. Beginners should read the introduction to the crust chapter, which includes step-by-step instructions for preparing and rolling out pie dough as well as finishing and decorating a pie. (Experienced bakers may wish to substitute their favorite pie crust for the suggested recipe or to select another compatible crust from among the many recipes.)
- Chilling the dough: Anyone who has made a lot of pie crusts will testify that no two crusts act alike. Depending on humidity, temperature, age of the flour, and condition of the shortening, a pie crust may shape up magically or prove a very stubborn subject. Butter crusts almost always benefit from a minimum of 30 minutes of chilling in the refrigerator and a chilled marble slab for rolling out, but even vegetable shortening can act up on a hot day. A quick way to stabilize sticky dough is to chill it in the freezer for 15 to 20 minutes. The second half of the dough for a double-crust pie should always be refrigerated while the filling is prepared.
- The amount of juice in a fruit pie depends on the type of filling used. Pies made with apples contain a large amount of pectin, a natural jelling agent found in that fruit; cherry pies, which have no pectin, are almost always very juicy. To keep the bottom crust of a juicy pie from becoming soggy, paint with egg white or sprinkle with a little flour before adding the filling.
- Beaten egg yolk, egg white, or milk applied to the top crust with a pastry brush before baking make excellent pie glazes.
- Leftover dough may be turned into turnovers, tartlets, or delightfully flaky jam rolls. To make a jam roll, gather up leftover scraps of dough into a ball and roll out to an ⅛-inch thickness. Paint the surface of the dough thinly with jam (raspberry is excellent) and roll up the dough, just like a rug. Place the jam roll on an ungreased baking sheet and bake together with the pie. Check the pastry after 10 minutes and continue to bake until golden brown. Cool, and cut into 1-inch slices. The length of time required for baking a jam roll depends on the oven temperature given for the specific pie.
- Freezing: Well-wrapped, unbaked pie shells may be frozen for up to 6 months. There is no need to defrost a frozen pie shell before baking. Unbaked dough also may be frozen, but should be defrosted to cool room temperature before rolling out.

- How many servings are there in a 9-inch pie? There are six to eight, depending on the size of the slice and the richness of the pie. To serve a pie, first cut it in half, using a sharp knife. Then, slice a wedge to the desired size. Use a pie server or spatula to lift the wedge from the pie plate. The first slice of a pie is almost never perfect in appearance.
- Serving and storing pies: Almost any pie is at its best when eaten no more than a few hours after its creation. All custard and gelatin pies must be refrigerated until serving to prevent spoilage; fruit pies are best warm or at room temperature; main course pies are served either hot or warm. Leftover fruit pie becomes soggy when refrigerated. To store, cover and keep at room temperature.

From tart lemon and cool, velvety chocolate cream to fresh cherry and the first crisp apple pie of autumn, homemade pies are always in season and always appreciated. Whether you're a first-time baker or an experienced and creative cook, *Great Pies You Can Bake* makes pie baking a treat—after all, it's just as easy as pie.

Crusts

Here is a step-by-step guide to making the perfect pie crust. First, check the ingredients list of the recipe for the suggested crust (the Classic Apple Pie uses the Classic Double Crust, for example). Then, prepare the dough using the crust recipe in this chapter. Follow the instructions for rolling out the dough, and finish the pie as directed in the recipe.

Rolling Out the Dough

Place the chilled dough on a lightly floured bread board or chilled marble slab. (A lightly floured canvas pastry cloth and rolling-pin sleeve will greatly facilitate rolling out the dough.) Flatten the dough with a floured rolling pin. Working from the center out, roll out the dough to an ⅛-inch thickness. The diameter of the dough circle should be about 2 inches greater than the pie—11 inches for a standard 9-inch pie pan. Drape the dough over the rolling pin (if you are not using a pastry cloth, first gently loosen the dough from the bread board with a spatula) and carefully transfer to the pie pan. Depending on the type of pie—single crust, double crust, lattice-top, decorated-top, or prebaked shell—refer to the following instructions for finishing the pie crust.

Single-Crust Pie

For a single-crust pie, cut off any crust in excess of 2 inches beyond the pie pan, using a sharp knife or a scissors. Turning the dough from the bottom upward, roll up the edges of the pie. Crimp the pie around the rim, making a fluted edge with two thumbs pressed together. Fill and bake as directed in the recipe.

Double-Crust Pie

For a double-crust pie, leave the bottom crust untrimmed (do not crimp). Fill the pie, then roll out the top crust. Place the top crust over the filling. Trim off any crust in excess of 2 inches beyond the pie pan. Turning the double layer of dough from the bottom upward, roll up the edges of the pie. Crimp the pie around the rim, making a fluted edge with two thumbs pressed together. Using the tines of a fork, prick vents in the top of the pie for steam to escape (a sun pattern is easy and attractive; you can also cut short vents with a knife or scissors), otherwise the pie may crack while it is baking. Bake as directed in the recipe.

Lattice-Top Pie

For a lattice-top pie, leave the bottom crust untrimmed (do not crimp). Fill the pie, then roll out the top crust, making it slightly thicker than the bottom crust. Using a sharp knife or pastry wheel, cut the crust into ½-inch strips. Lay half of the strips across the pie, spacing ¾ inch apart. Bending back alternate strips, interweave the remaining strips to form a diamond pattern. Connect the ends of the strips to the crust, allowing a little slack for shrinkage. Turning the dough from the bottom upward, roll up the edges of the pie. Crimp the pie around the rim, making a fluted edge with two thumbs pressed together. Sprinkle 1 tablespoon of sugar over the top and bake as directed in the recipe; you can also brush the unbaked lattice with beaten egg.

Fancy Cut-Out Crust or Patterned Top

For a cut-out crust, leave the bottom crust untrimmed (do not crimp). Fill the pie, then roll out the top crust, making it slightly thicker than the bottom crust. Using a small biscuit or cookie cutter, carefully punch out an attractive design from the top crust. Place the crust on top of the filling and finish as for a double-crust pie. Bake as directed in the recipe.

For a patterned top, cut out fanciful shapes from the dough and arrange them on top of the pie filling. Do not leave too much open space or the pie may dry out. Bake as directed in the recipe.

CLASSIC DOUBLE CRUST

Two 9-inch pie crusts

2½ cups sifted all-purpose
　　flour
½ teaspoon salt

¾ cup solid vegetable
　　shortening (Crisco®)
6 to 7 tablespoons ice water

Sift together the flour and salt. Add ½ cup of the shortening to the flour mixture. Using a pastry blender, cut the shortening into the flour until the mixture has the texture of cornmeal. Add the remaining shortening and cut until the mixture is the size of small peas. Add the water, 1 tablespoon at a time, while tossing the mixture with a fork. Add only enough water to make the dough particles stick together. Press the dough into a ball and cut the ball in half. Wrap each half in waxed paper and chill until ready to use.

CLASSIC SINGLE CRUST

One 9-inch pie crust

1½ cups sifted all-purpose
　　flour
¼ teaspoon salt

½ cup solid vegetable
　　shortening (Crisco®)
2 to 3 tablespoons ice water

Sift together the flour and salt. Add the shortening to the flour mixture. Using a pastry blender, cut the shortening into the flour until the mixture has the texture of cornmeal. Add the water, 1 tablespoon at a time, while tossing the mixture with a fork. Add only enough water to make the dough particles stick together. Press the dough into a ball. Wrap in waxed paper and chill until ready to use.

PREBAKED PIE SHELL
One 9-inch pie shell

Follow the recipe for Classic Single Crust. Roll out the dough. Line a 9-inch pie pan with dough. Trim and crimp the edges.

Preheat the oven to 450° F. Prick the bottom of the crust with the tines of a fork. Line the shell with waxed paper or baking parchment, and fill with baking weights such as dried beans or aluminum pellets. Bake 10 minutes. Remove the beans and waxed paper and return the pie shell to the oven. Bake 2 minutes more or until lightly browned.

CHEDDAR CHEESE CRUST
One 9-inch pie crust

Follow the recipe for Classic Single Crust, adding ½ cup of grated cheddar cheese to the flour mixture.

BAKING POWDER CRUST
One 9-inch crust
with leftover dough for biscuits

2 cups sifted all-purpose flour	¾ cup unsalted butter or margarine, chilled and
½ teaspoon salt	cut into pieces
½ teaspoon baking powder	¼ cup cold milk

Sift together the flour, salt, and baking powder. Using a pastry blender, cut the butter into the flour until the mixture has the texture of cornmeal. Add the milk, 1 tablespoon at a time, while tossing the mixture with a fork. Add only enough milk to make the dough particles stick together. Press the dough into a ball. Wrap in waxed paper and chill until ready to use. Leftover dough may be used for biscuits or jam rolls (see page vii).

BUTTER CRUST

One 9-inch pie crust
Double recipe for two 9-inch pie crusts

1½ cups sifted all-purpose
    flour
¼ teaspoon salt

¾ cup unsalted butter,
    chilled and cut into
    pieces
3 tablespoons ice water

Sift together the flour and salt. Using a pastry blender, cut the butter into the flour until the mixture has the texture of cornmeal. Add the water, 1 tablespoon at a time, while tossing the mixture with a fork. Add only enough water to make the dough particles stick together. Press the dough into a ball. Wrap in waxed paper and chill until ready to use. Best if chilled at least 30 minutes.

PREBAKED QUICHE SHELL

One 9-inch quiche shell

Follow the recipe for Butter Crust. Roll out the dough. Line a 9-inch quiche pan with dough. Trim and crimp the edges.

Preheat the oven to 400° F. Prick the bottom of the crust with the tines of a fork. Line the shell with waxed paper, and fill with baking weights such as dried beans or aluminum pellets. Bake 15 minutes. Remove the beans and waxed paper and return to the oven. Bake 5 minutes more or until lightly browned.

CHOCOLATE CRUST

One 9-inch pie crust
Double recipe for two 9-inch pie crusts

1½ cups sifted all-purpose
    flour
2 tablespoons unsweetened
    cocoa powder
¼ teaspoon salt

1 tablespoon sugar
½ cup solid vegetable
    shortening (Crisco®)
3 to 4 tablespoons ice water

Sift together the flour, cocoa, salt, and sugar. Using a pastry blender, cut the shortening into the flour mixture until it has the texture of cornmeal. Add the water, 1 tablespoon at a time, while tossing the mixture with a fork. Add only enough water to make the dough particles stick together. Press the dough into a ball. Wrap in waxed paper and chill until ready to use.

EGG CRUST
Two 9-inch pie crusts

2 cups plus 2 tablespoons
    sifted all-purpose flour
2 teaspoons sugar
1 teaspoon salt
¾ cup plus 2 tablespoons
    solid vegetable
    shortening (Crisco®)

¼ cup cold water
1 teaspoon cider vinegar
1 egg, beaten

Sift together the flour, sugar, and salt. Using a pastry blender, cut the shortening into the flour mixture until it has the texture of cornmeal. Combine the water, vinegar, and egg and add to the flour mixture while tossing the mixture with a fork. Press the dough into a ball and cut the ball in half. Wrap each half in waxed paper and chill for at least 30 minutes. (Note: This dough is very sticky when first mixed but firms up after chilling.)

LEMON CRUST
Two 9-inch pie crusts

Follow the recipe for Egg Crust, substituting lemon juice for vinegar and adding 2 teaspoons of grated lemon zest to the egg mixture.

ORANGE CRUST
Two 9-inch pie crusts

Follow the recipe for Egg Crust, substituting orange juice for vinegar and adding 2 teaspoons of grated orange zest to the egg mixture.

GRAHAM CRACKER CRUST

One 9-inch pie crust

2 cups crushed graham   ¾ cup unsalted butter or
    crackers, firmly packed   margarine, melted

Preheat the oven to 375° F. Combine the graham crackers and butter. Mix well. Press the mixture firmly into the bottom and up the sides of the pie pan. Bake 8 minutes.

CHOCOLATE WAFER CRUST

One 9-inch pie crust

2 cups crushed chocolate   ¾ cup unsalted butter or
    wafers, firmly packed   margarine, melted

Preheat the oven to 375° F. Combine the chocolate wafers and butter. Mix well. Press the mixture firmly into the bottom and up the sides of the pie pan. Bake 8 minutes.

GINGERSNAP CRUST

One 9-inch pie crust

2 cups crushed gingersnaps,   ¾ cup unsalted butter or
    firmly packed   margarine, melted

Preheat the oven to 375° F. Combine the gingersnaps and butter. Mix well. Press the mixture firmly into the bottom and up the sides of the pie pan. Bake 8 minutes.

VANILLA WAFER CRUST

One 9-inch pie crust

2 cups crushed vanilla   ¾ cup unsalted butter or
    wafers, firmly packed   margarine, melted

Preheat the oven to 375° F. Combine the vanilla wafers and butter. Mix well. Press the mixture firmly into the bottom and up the sides of the pie pan. Bake 8 minutes.

MERINGUE CRUST

One 9-inch pie crust

4 large egg whites
⅛ teaspoon salt
½ teaspoon cream of tartar

1 teaspoon vanilla extract
¼ teaspoon almond extract
1 cup superfine sugar

Preheat the oven to 275° F. Cut out a single sheet of waxed paper or baking parchment to fit the bottom and sides of the pie pan. Thoroughly butter the paper and insert in the pan, buttered side up.

Beat the egg whites until they form stiff peaks. Beat in the salt, cream of tartar, vanilla, and almond extract. Beat for 1 minute. Beat in the sugar, ⅓ cup at a time. Carefully spread the meringue on the buttered paper to the thickness of 2 inches. Bake 50 minutes. Turn off the heat and let the oven cool before removing the pie shell. Carefully remove the waxed paper from the cooled meringue.

SWEET CRUST

One 9-inch pie crust
Double recipe for two 9-inch pie crusts

1½ cups sifted all-purpose
    flour
¼ teaspoon salt
1 tablespoon sugar

½ cup unsalted butter,
    chilled and cut into
    pieces
3 to 4 tablespoons ice water

Sift together the flour, salt, and sugar. Using a pastry blender, cut butter into the flour mixture until it has the texture of cornmeal. Add the water, 1 tablespoon at a time, while tossing the mixture with a fork. Add only enough water to make the dough particles stick together. Press the dough into a ball. Wrap in waxed paper and chill until ready to use. Best if chilled at least 30 minutes.

PREBAKED SWEET CRUST
OR TART SHELL

One 9-inch shell

Follow the recipe for Sweet Crust. Roll out the dough. Line the pie or tart pan with dough. Trim and crimp the edges.

Preheat the oven to 400° F. Prick the bottom of the crust with the tines of a fork. Line the shell with waxed paper, and fill with baking weights such as dried beans or aluminum pellets. Bake 15 minutes. Remove the beans and waxed paper and return to the oven. Bake 5 minutes more or until lightly browned.

SPICE CRUST

One 9-inch pie crust
Double recipe for two 9-inch pie crusts

1½ cups sifted all-purpose
    flour
¼ teaspoon salt
2 teaspoons sugar
½ teaspoon cinnamon

½ teaspoon nutmeg
½ cup unsalted butter,
    chilled and cut into
    pieces
3 to 4 tablespoons ice water

Sift together the flour, salt, sugar, cinnamon, and nutmeg. Using a pastry blender, cut the butter into the flour mixture until it has the texture of cornmeal. Add the water, 1 tablespoon at a time, while tossing the mixture with a fork. Add only enough water to make the dough particles stick together. Press the dough into a ball. Wrap in waxed paper and chill until ready to use. Best if chilled at least 30 minutes.

WALNUT CRUST

One 9-inch pie crust
Double recipe for two 9-inch pie crusts

1½ cups sifted all-purpose
    flour
⅛ teaspoon salt
¼ cup ground walnuts

½ cup unsalted butter,
    chilled and cut into
    pieces
3 to 4 tablespoons ice water

Combine the flour, salt, and walnuts. Using a pastry blender, cut the butter into the flour mixture until it has the texture of cornmeal. Add the water, 1 tablespoon at a time, while tossing the mixture with a fork. Add only enough water to make the dough particles stick together. Press the dough into a ball and cut the ball in half. Wrap each half in waxed paper and chill until ready to use. Best if chilled at least 30 minutes.

Apple Pies

A slice of warm apple pie, scented with cinnamon and lemon and accompanied by vanilla ice cream, is the substance of many fond memories. This all-American dish, which comes in many forms and flavors, richly rewards the patience of the apple peeler. There are many different varieties of apples available, and each lends a unique and distinctive presence to a pie. A good rule of thumb is that the sweeter the fruit, the less sugar is needed. Firm, fresh apples of any sort are always preferable to waxed, cold-storage fruit. Lemon juice squeezed over the peeled apple slices will prevent browning while the crust is prepared. Most spices may be adjusted to taste.

CLASSIC APPLE PIE

One 9-inch double-crust pie

Pastry for a 9-inch double-crust pie
(Classic Double Crust)

½ cup sugar
½ teaspoon cinnamon
⅛ teaspoon nutmeg
⅛ teaspoon salt
1 tablespoon cornstarch
½ teaspoon grated lemon
    zest

5 cups peeled, cored, and
    thinly sliced tart apples
1 tablespoon lemon juice
1½ tablespoons unsalted
    butter or margarine

Preheat the oven to 450° F. Prepare the pie pastry. Line the pie pan with the bottom crust, using half of the dough. Keep the remaining dough chilled.

Combine the sugar, cinnamon, nutmeg, salt, cornstarch, and lemon zest. Add the apples and lemon juice. Mix well. Turn the filling into the crust and dot with butter. Roll out the top crust and lay it on the filling. Trim off any excess dough, crimp the edges, and prick with the tines of a fork to vent.

Bake at 450° F for 10 minutes. Reduce the heat to 350° F and bake about 45 minutes more or until golden brown.

CHEESE-TOPPED APPLE PIE

One 9-inch double-crust pie

Follow the recipe for Classic Apple Pie (No. 1). Just before serving, cover the top crust of the baked apple pie with thin slices of sharp cheddar cheese. Turn on the broiler and return the pie to the oven just long enough to melt the cheese. Serve immediately.

NO. 3   **APPLE CRANBERRY PIE**

One 9-inch double-crust pie

Pastry for a 9-inch double-crust pie
(Classic Double Crust)

¾ cup dark brown sugar,   4 cups peeled, cored, and
   firmly packed   thinly sliced tart apples
¼ cup sugar   2 cups whole cranberries
⅓ cup flour   2 tablespoons unsalted
1 teaspoon allspice   butter or margarine
1 teaspoon grated orange
   zest

Preheat the oven to 425° F. Prepare the pie pastry. Line the pie
pan with the bottom crust, using half of the dough. Keep the
remaining dough chilled.

Combine the sugars, flour, allspice, and orange zest. Add the
apples and cranberries. Mix well. Turn the filling into the crust
and dot with butter. Roll out the top crust and lay it on the filling.
Trim off any excess dough, crimp the edges, and prick with the
tines of a fork to vent.

Bake 40 minutes or until golden brown.

NO. 4   **LATTICE-TOP APPLE
                                   CRANBERRY PIE**

One 9-inch lattice-top pie

Pastry for a 9-inch lattice-top pie
(Classic Double Crust)

1 cup plus 1 tablespoon   2 tablespoons mincemeat
   sugar   1 teaspoon grated lemon
2 tablespoons flour   zest
4 cups peeled, cored, and   ⅛ teaspoon salt
   thinly sliced tart apples   2 tablespoons water
1 cup chopped cranberries

Preheat the oven to 450° F. Prepare the pie pastry. Line the pie
pan with the bottom crust, using half of the dough. Keep the
remaining dough chilled.

Combine 1 cup of the sugar with the flour. Sprinkle one fourth
of the sugar mixture evenly over the bottom crust. Combine the
apples, cranberries, mincemeat, lemon zest, and salt. Mix well. Stir
in the water and turn the filling into the pie shell. Cover with the

remaining sugar mixture. Roll out, cut, and lay on the lattice strips. After the pie is latticed and crimped, sprinkle 1 tablespoon of sugar over the lattice crust.

Bake at 450° F for 10 minutes. Reduce the heat to 350° F and bake about 30 minutes more or until golden brown.

NO. 5

APPLE CRUMB PIE
One 9-inch single-crust pie

Pastry for a 9-inch single-crust pie
(Classic Single Crust)

½ cup sugar
1 teaspoon cinnamon
½ teaspoon mace
5 cups peeled, cored, and thinly sliced tart apples

⅓ cup light brown sugar, firmly packed
¾ cup flour
6 tablespoons unsalted butter or margarine
Sweetened whipped cream

Preheat the oven to 400° F. Prepare the pie pastry. Line the pie pan with the dough. Trim and crimp the edges.

Combine the sugar, cinnamon, and mace. Add the apples. Mix well. Turn the filling into the crust. In another bowl, mix together the brown sugar and flour. Using a pastry blender or the tines of a fork, cut in the butter until the mixture is crumbly. Sprinkle the crumbs evenly over the filling.

Bake 35 to 40 minutes or until golden brown. Serve with sweetened whipped cream.

NO. 6

APPLE CUSTARD PIE
One 9-inch single-crust pie

Pastry for a 9-inch single-crust pie
(Classic Single Crust)

6 large sweet apples, peeled, cored, and quartered
1 cup sugar
½ teaspoon cinnamon
¼ teaspoon nutmeg

⅛ teaspoon salt
2 eggs
½ cup milk
½ cup heavy cream

Preheat the oven to 450° F. Prepare the pie pastry. Line the pie pan with the dough. Trim and crimp the edges.

Reduce the apples to a fine pulp in a food processor. Add the sugar, cinnamon, nutmeg, and salt. Process to mix well. In a large bowl, beat the eggs until foamy. Stir in the milk and cream, then combine with the apple mixture. Turn the filling into the crust.

Bake at 450° F for 10 minutes. Reduce the heat to 350° F and bake about 40 minutes more. Cool, and refrigerate if not serving immediately.

NO. 7   **APPLE MERINGUE PIE**

One 9-inch single-crust pie

Pastry for a 9-inch single-crust pie
(Classic Single Crust)

5 cups peeled, cored, and thinly sliced tart apples	1 teaspoon cinnamon
2 cups water	1 teaspoon allspice
¼ cup light brown sugar, firmly packed	1 tablespoon lemon juice
	1 teaspoon grated lemon zest

Meringue

3 large egg whites, at room temperature	¼ teaspoon cream of tartar
½ teaspoon vanilla extract	6 tablespoons superfine sugar

Preheat the oven to 450° F. Prepare the pie pastry. Line the pie pan with the dough. Trim and crimp the edges.

Bring the water to a boil in a large saucepan. Add the apples and simmer over low heat until tender. Drain well and combine with the brown sugar, cinnamon, allspice, lemon juice, and lemon zest. Turn the filling into the crust.

Bake at 450° F for 20 to 25 minutes. Remove the pie from the oven, and reduce the heat to 350° F.

While the pie is still hot, prepare the meringue. Beat the egg whites, vanilla, and cream of tartar until the mixture holds stiff peaks. Gradually add the sugar, 1 tablespoon at a time, beating until very stiff and glossy. All the sugar must be dissolved. Spread the meringue over the pie filling, sealing it to the edge of the crust. Bake 12 to 15 minutes or until golden brown.

NO. 8

APPLE PIE CAKE

One 9-inch "pie"

½ cup sugar
2½ cups sifted flour
2 teaspoons baking powder
1 cup unsalted butter or margarine
2 egg yolks
1 tablespoon grated lemon zest

½ teaspoon vanilla extract
2 tablespoons whiskey
5 cups peeled, cored, and thinly sliced tart apples
1 teaspoon cinnamon
½ teaspoon nutmeg
½ cup brown sugar
2 egg whites

Preheat the oven to 400° F. Lightly grease a large baking sheet with butter or vegetable shortening.

Combine the sugar, flour, and baking powder. Using a pastry blender, cut in the butter until the mixture has the texture of cornmeal. Mix together the egg yolks, lemon zest, vanilla, and whiskey. Add the egg mixture to the flour mixture and stir well. Press the dough into a ball. Cut the dough ball in half, wrap each half in waxed paper, and chill for at least 20 minutes.

When the dough is chilled, roll out one half onto plastic wrap lightly dusted with flour. Transfer the dough circle to the baking sheet. Arrange the apples in the middle of the dough circle. Mix together the cinnamon, nutmeg, and brown sugar. Sprinkle the sugar mixture on top of the apples. Roll out the remaining dough and cover the top of the pie. Trim off any excess dough, crimp the edges, and prick with the tines of a fork to vent. Brush with egg white.

Reduce the heat to 350° F and bake 45 to 60 minutes or until golden brown.

NO. 9

APPLESAUCE MERINGUE PIE

One 9-inch single-crust pie

**Pastry for a 9-inch single-crust pie
(Classic Single Crust)**

2 cups unsweetened applesauce
¾ cup sugar
⅛ teaspoon salt
3 egg yolks

1 cup milk
1 tablespoon unsalted butter or margarine, melted
1 teaspoon lemon juice
2 teaspoons grated lemon zest

Meringue

3 large egg whites, at room   ¼ teaspoon cream of tartar
    temperature   6 tablespoons superfine
½ teaspoon vanilla extract   sugar

Preheat the oven to 450° F. Prepare the pie pastry. Line the pie pan with the dough. Trim and crimp the edges.

Combine the applesauce, sugar, and salt. In a separate bowl, beat the egg yolks until foamy. Stir in the milk. Combine the egg mixture with the applesauce mixture. Add the melted butter, lemon juice, and lemon zest. Turn the filling into the crust.

Bake at 450° F for 10 minutes. Reduce the heat to 350° F and bake 35 minutes more. Remove the pie from the oven and leave the oven on.

While the pie is still hot, prepare the meringue. Beat the egg whites, vanilla, and cream of tartar until the mixture holds stiff peaks. Gradually add the sugar, 1 tablespoon at a time, beating until very stiff and glossy. All the sugar must be dissolved. Spread the meringue over the pie filling, sealing it to the edge of the crust. Bake 12 to 15 minutes or until golden brown.

NO. 10   **CALVADOS APPLE PIE**

One 9-inch lattice-top pie

Pastry for a 9-inch lattice-top pie
(Classic Double Crust)

½ cup plus 1 tablespoon   3 tablespoons Calvados
    sugar   liqueur or brandy
2 tablespoons dark brown   4 cups peeled, cored, and
    sugar, firmly packed   thinly sliced tart apples
1 teaspoon cinnamon   1 tablespoon lemon juice
½ teaspoon nutmeg   Sweetened whipped cream
2 teaspoons grated lemon
    zest

Preheat the oven to 450° F. Prepare the pie pastry. Line the pie pan with the bottom crust, using half of the dough. Keep the remaining dough chilled.

Combine ½ cup of the sugar, brown sugar, cinnamon, nutmeg, lemon zest, and Calvados. Add the apples and lemon juice. Mix well. Turn the filling in the crust. Roll out, cut, and lay on the lattice strips. After the pie is latticed and crimped, sprinkle 1 tablespoon of sugar over the lattice crust.

Place the pie on the bottom rack of the oven and bake for 10 minutes. Reduce the heat to 350° F and bake 25 minutes more or until golden brown. Serve warm, with sweetened whipped cream.

NO. 11

CIDER APPLE PIE

One 9-inch lattice-top pie

Pastry for a 9-inch lattice-top pie
(Classic Double Crust)

6 medium-size tart apples, peeled, cored, and cut into eighths
1 cup apple cider
1 to 2 tablespoons flour (optional)

½ cup plus 1 tablespoon sugar
1 teaspoon cinnamon
¼ teaspoon nutmeg
⅛ teaspoon ground cloves
⅛ teaspoon salt

Preheat the oven to 450° F. Prepare the pie pastry. Line the pie pan with the bottom crust, using half of the dough. Keep the remaining dough chilled.

Combine the apples and cider in a saucepan. Cook, over low heat, about 30 minutes or until the apples are tender. Remove the pan from the heat. If the mixture seems too thin, add 1 to 2 tablespoons of flour to thicken it, first stirring a little of the cooking liquid into the flour before adding it to the pan. Stir in ½ cup sugar, cinnamon, nutmeg, cloves, and salt. Mix well. Turn the filling into the crust. Roll out, cut, and lay on the lattice strips. After the pie is latticed and crimped, sprinkle 1 tablespoon of sugar over the lattice crust.

Bake at 450° F for 10 minutes. Reduce the heat to 350° F and bake 25 minutes more or until golden brown.

NO. 12

CRAB APPLE PIE

One 9-inch double-crust pie

Pastry for a 9-inch double-crust pie
(Classic Double Crust)

3 cups peeled, cored, and quartered crab apples
1½ cups light brown sugar, firmly packed

1 tablespoon flour
1 teaspoon cinnamon
1 tablespoon lemon juice
1 tablespoon water

Preheat the oven to 450° F. Prepare the pie pastry. Line the pie pan with the bottom crust, using half of the dough. Keep the remaining dough chilled.

Arrange the crab apples in the crust. Combine the sugar, flour, and cinnamon and sprinkle over the crab apples. Combine the lemon juice and water and sprinkle over the sugar. Roll out the top crust and lay it on the filling. Trim off any excess dough, crimp the edges, and prick with the tines of a fork to vent.

Bake at 450° F for 10 minutes. Reduce the heat to 350° F and bake about 40 minutes more or until golden brown.

NO. 13   **DEEP-DISH APPLE PIE**

One 9-inch single-crust pie

**Pastry for a 9-inch single-crust pie
(Baking Powder Crust)**

¾ cup sugar

⅛ teaspoon salt

½ teaspoon nutmeg

½ teaspoon cinnamon

5 cups peeled, cored, and
    thinly sliced sweet
    apples

1 tablespoon lemon juice

2 tablespoons unsalted
    butter or margarine

Ice cream

Preheat the oven to 425° F. Prepare the pie pastry. Keep the dough chilled until the filling is ready.

Combine the sugar, salt, nutmeg, and cinnamon. Add the apples and lemon juice and mix until well coated. Thoroughly butter the bottom and sides of a 9-inch deep-dish pie pan. Turn the filling into the pan and dot with butter. Roll out the pastry and lay it on the filling. Trim off any excess dough, crimp the edges, and prick with the tines of a fork to vent.

Bake about 30 minutes or until golden brown. Serve plain or with ice cream.

NO. 14

GREEN APPLE PIE

One 9-inch double-crust pie

Pastry for a 9-inch double-crust pie
(Classic Double Crust)

1 cup dark brown sugar, firmly packed	8 to 12 small green apples, peeled, cored, and thinly sliced
1 tablespoon flour	
⅛ teaspoon salt	2 tablespoons unsalted butter or margarine
½ teaspoon nutmeg	

Preheat the oven to 450° F. Prepare the pie pastry. Line the pie pan with the bottom crust, using half of the dough. Keep the remaining dough chilled.

Combine the sugar, flour, salt, and nutmeg. Sprinkle one fourth of the sugar mixture evenly over the bottom of the crust. Layer the apples in the crust, piling up pieces toward the center of the pie. Cover with the remaining sugar mixture and dot with butter. Roll out the top crust and lay it on the filling. Trim off any excess dough, crimp the edges, and prick with the tines of a fork to vent.

Bake at 450° F for 10 minutes. Reduce the heat to 350° F and bake 40 minutes more or until golden brown.

NO. 15

CHEESE-CRUST GREEN APPLE PIE

One 9-inch double-crust pie

Follow the recipe for Green Apple Pie (No. 14), substituting a double recipe of the Cheddar Cheese Crust for the Classic Double Crust. Serve warm.

NO. 16   **HONEY APPLE PIE**

One 9-inch single-crust pie

**Pastry for a 9-inch single-crust pie
(Classic Single Crust)**

5 cups peeled, cored, and thinly sliced tart apples	2 tablespoons unsalted butter or margarine
½ cup sugar	½ cup honey
1 tablespoon uncooked tapioca	¼ cup heavy cream
½ teaspoon cinnamon	⅓ cup pecans, coarsely chopped
⅛ teaspoon salt	

Preheat the oven to 450° F. Prepare the pie pastry. Line the pie pan with the dough. Trim and crimp the edges.

Combine the apples with the sugar, tapioca, cinnamon, and salt. Arrange the apples in the crust and dot with butter.

Bake at 450° F for 10 minutes. Reduce the heat to 350° F. Cover with an inverted lightweight pie pan and bake for 20 minutes. Remove the cover and bake 15 minutes more or until the apples are tender.

Remove the pie from the oven. Mix the honey with the cream. Drizzle the honey mixture over the hot pie and sprinkle on the pecans. Serve warm.

NO. 17   **MARLBORO PIE**

One 9-inch single-crust pie

**Pastry for a 9-inch single-crust pie
(Classic Single Crust)**

6 large tart apples, peeled, cored, and cut into eighths	3 eggs, lightly beaten
¼ cup water	2 teaspoons grated lemon zest
¼ cup unsalted butter or margarine, cut into pieces	2 tablespoons lemon juice
¾ cup sugar	1½ tablespoons dry sherry
	⅛ teaspoon salt

Preheat the oven to 450° F. Prepare the pie pastry. Line the pie pan with the dough. Trim and crimp the edges.

Combine the apples and water in a large saucepan. Cook, over low heat, for about 30 minutes or until the apples are tender.

Remove the pan from the heat. Reduce the apples to a fine pulp in a food processor, then remove to a bowl. Stir the butter into the hot pulp. Add the sugar, eggs, lemon zest, lemon juice, sherry, and salt. Mix well. Turn the filling into the crust.

Bake at 450° F for 10 minutes. Reduce the heat to 325° F and bake 30 minutes more.

NO. 18

MT. VERNON APPLE PIE

One 9-inch single-crust pie

**Pastry for a 9-inch single-crust pie
(Classic Single Crust)**

6 large tart apples, peeled, cored, and cut into eighths
¼ cup water
½ cup sugar
½ teaspoon cinnamon
⅛ teaspoon salt
½ cup cake or cookie crumbs

3 tablespoons unsalted butter or margarine, melted
2 eggs, lightly beaten
2 tablespoons lemon juice
2 teaspoons grated lemon zest
Sweetened whipped cream

Preheat the oven to 450° F. Prepare the pie pastry. Line the pie pan with the dough. Trim and crimp the edges.

Combine the apples and water in a large saucepan. Cook, over low heat, for about 30 minutes or until the apples are tender. Remove the pan from the heat. Reduce the apples to a fine pulp in a food processor, then remove to a bowl. Stir in the sugar, cinnamon, and salt. Combine the cake crumbs with the melted butter and add to the mixture. Stir in the eggs, lemon juice, and lemon zest. Turn the filling into the crust.

Bake at 450° F for 10 minutes. Reduce the heat to 350° F and bake 30 minutes more. Cool slightly, cover with sweetened whipped cream, and serve.

NO. 19   **OPEN-FACE APPLE**
                                                          PIE I

One 9-inch single-crust pie

Pastry for a 9-inch single-crust pie
(Classic Single Crust)

1 cup light brown sugar,	⅛ teaspoon salt
firmly packed	5 cups peeled, cored, and
2 tablespoons flour	thinly sliced tart apples
¼ teaspoon nutmeg	1 cup sour cream
½ teaspoon allspice	

Preheat the oven to 450° F. Prepare the pie pastry. Line the pie
pan with the dough. Trim and crimp the edges.

Combine the sugar, flour, nutmeg, allspice, and salt. Sprinkle
one fourth of the sugar mixture over the bottom of the crust.
Arrange the apples in the crust in concentric layers. Top with the
remaining sugar mixture.

Bake at 450° F for 10 minutes. Reduce the heat to 350° F.
Cover with an inverted lightweight pie pan and bake for 15 minutes.
Remove the cover and add the sour cream. Bake 25 minutes more.
Serve warm.

NO. 20   **OPEN-FACE APPLE**
                                                         PIE II

One 9-inch single-crust pie

Pastry for a 9-inch single-crust pie
(Classic Single Crust)

½ cup light brown sugar,	2 tablespoons flour
firmly packed	5 cups peeled, cored, and
½ teaspoon cinnamon	thinly sliced sweet
¼ teaspoon nutmeg	apples
⅛ teaspoon salt	¼ cup unsalted butter or
1 teaspoon grated lemon	margarine, melted
zest	¼ cup sugar

Preheat the oven to 450° F. Prepare the pie pastry. Line the pie
pan with the dough. Trim and crimp the edges.

Combine the brown sugar, cinnamon, nutmeg, salt, lemon zest,
and flour. Add the apples and mix well. Arrange the apples in the
crust in concentric circles. Pour the melted butter over the apples

and sprinkle with sugar.

Bake at 450° F for 10 minutes. Reduce the heat to 350° F. Cover with an inverted lightweight pie pan and bake 35 minutes more.

NO. 21

GLAZED OPEN-FACE APPLE PIE

One 9-inch single-crust pie

Follow the recipe for Open-Face Apple Pie II (No. 20), reserving the apple peelings for the glaze. Glaze the pie as soon as it is removed from the oven. To prepare the glaze, combine the apple peelings, ½ cup water and 1 cup sugar in a large saucepan. Bring the mixture to a boil and cook over low heat, stirring frequently, until a heavy syrup is formed. Remove the pan from the heat, strain, and pour the glaze over the hot pie. Cool before serving.

NO. 22

PEACHY APPLE PIE

One 9-inch single-crust pie

**Prebaked 9-inch pie shell
(Classic Single Crust or
Graham Cracker Crust)**
  1 cup sugar
  ½ cup plus 2 tablespoons
    water
  5 cups peeled, cored, and
    thinly sliced tart apples

  1 teaspoon cornstarch
  2 tablespoons lemon juice
  1 tablespoon brandy
  ½ cup peach jam
  ¼ cup chopped candied
    citron

Prepare the prebaked pie shell; cool completely.

Preheat the oven to 350° F. Combine the sugar and ½ cup water in a large saucepan. Add the apples and cook, over low heat, until the slices are tender but still hold their shape. Cool and drain the apples, reserving the syrup. Arrange the apples in the pie shell in concentric circles. Mix the cornstarch with 2 tablespoons of water and add to the syrup. Cook, over low heat, until the syrup is clear. Remove the pan from the heat. Add the lemon juice and brandy and mix well. Pour the syrup over the apples. Spread the peach jam over the apples and sprinkle with citron.

Bake 15 minutes.

NO. 23   **PENNSYLVANIA DUTCH**
                                          APPLE PIE

One 9-inch single-crust pie

Pastry for a 9-inch single-crust pie
(Classic Single Crust)
  1 tablespoon flour
  ⅛ teaspoon salt
  1 cup sugar
  ¼ teaspoon nutmeg

  ½ teaspoon cinnamon, plus
     additional for decoration
  ¾ cup heavy cream
  5 cups peeled, cored, and
     thinly sliced tart apples

Preheat the oven to 450° F. Prepare the pie pastry. Line the pie pan with the dough. Trim and crimp the edges.

Combine the flour, salt, sugar, nutmeg, and ½ teaspoon of the cinnamon. Stir in the cream. Arrange the apples in the crust in concentric circles. Pour the cream mixture over the top.

Bake at 450° F for 10 minutes. Reduce the heat to 350° F. Cover with an inverted lightweight pie pan and bake 20 minutes. Remove the cover and bake 20 minutes more. Dust with cinnamon.

NO. 24   **REALLY RED APPLE PIE**

One 9-inch lattice-top pie

Pastry for a 9-inch lattice-top pie
(Classic Double Crust)
  1 cup sugar
  ½ cup water
  ⅓ cup cinnamon candy (red
     hots)
  2 drops red food coloring

  5 cups peeled, cored, and
     thinly sliced tart apples
  1 tablespoon flour
  1 teaspoon lemon juice
  1 tablespoon unsalted butter
     or margarine

Preheat the oven to 450° F. Prepare the pie pastry. Line the pie pan with the bottom crust, using half of the dough. Keep the remaining dough chilled.

In a saucepan, make a syrup by boiling the sugar, water, and candy until they are completely dissolved. Add the food coloring, then stir in the apples. Cook, over low heat, until the apples are bright red. Drain the apples, reserving ½ cup of the syrup. Stir some of the syrup into the flour, then blend back into the remaining syrup. Add the lemon juice and combine with the apples. Turn the filling into the crust and dot with butter. Roll out, cut, and lay on the lattice strips. After the pie is latticed and crimped, sprinkle 1 tablespoon of sugar over the lattice crust.

Bake at 450° F for 10 minutes. Reduce the heat to 375° F and bake about 20 minutes more or until golden brown.

NO. 25 **SCHNITZ PIE**

One 9-inch double-crust pie

Pastry for a 9-inch double-crust pie
(Classic Double Crust)

3 cups dried apples	2 teaspoons cinnamon
2 cups warm water	2 teaspoons grated orange
¼ cup orange juice	zest
1 cup dark brown sugar, firmly packed	½ teaspoon lemon extract

In a large saucepan, combine the apples with the warm water. Let the mixture stand for 30 minutes.

Preheat the oven to 450° F. Prepare the pie pastry. Line the pie pan with the bottom crust, using half of the dough. Keep the remaining dough chilled.

Add the orange juice to the apple mixture and bring to a boil. Reduce the heat and cook, stirring frequently, until the apples are tender. Remove the pan from the heat. Stir in the sugar, cinnamon, orange zest, and lemon extract. Mix well. Let the filling cool, then turn into the crust. Roll out the top crust and lay it on the filling. Trim off any excess dough, crimp the edges, and prick with the tines of a fork to vent.

Bake at 450° F for 10 minutes. Reduce the heat to 325° F and bake about 25 minutes more or until golden brown. Serve warm.

Fruit Pies

Nature certainly has provided well for the pie. These fruit pies draw heavily on the fresh produce of spring and summer in a celebration of the sweetness of the seasons and firm, juicy fruit that just cries out for a homemade pie. Out of season, drained canned fruit will do as a substitute, but nothing can replace the remarkable color and flavor of a fresh cherry pie. The fresher and sweeter the fruit is, the more extraordinary the pie will be. A cherry pitter is a welcome addition to basic pie-making utensils, and a light glaze of egg white added to the bottom (before filling) prevents the crust from getting soggy.

APRICOT PIE

One 9-inch lattice-top pie

**Pastry for a 9-inch lattice-top pie
(Classic Double Crust)**

⅓ cup flour

½ cup plus 1 tablespoon
    sugar

⅛ teaspoon nutmeg

4 cups halved, pitted
    apricots

1 tablespoon apricot nectar

1 tablespoon lemon juice

2 tablespoons unsalted
    butter or margarine

Preheat the oven to 450° F. Prepare the pie pastry. Line the pie pan with the bottom crust, using half of the dough. Keep the remaining dough chilled.

Combine the flour, sugar, and nutmeg. Sprinkle one fourth of the flour mixture evenly over the bottom of the crust. Arrange the apricots, with cut sides up, in concentric circles in the crust. Top with the remaining flour mixture. Combine the apricot nectar and lemon juice and sprinkle over the top. Dot with butter. Roll out, cut, and lay on the lattice strips. After the pie is latticed and crimped, sprinkle 1 tablespoon of sugar over the lattice crust.

Bake at 450° F for 10 minutes. Reduce the heat to 375° F and bake about 30 minutes more or until golden brown.

APRICOT MERINGUE PIE

One 9-inch single-crust pie

Recipe for Apricot Pie (No. 26)

Meringue

3 large egg whites, at room
    temperature

½ teaspoon vanilla extract

¼ teaspoon cream of tartar

6 tablespoons superfine
    sugar

Prepare the recipe for Apricot Pie, substituting the Classic Single Crust for the Classic Double Crust. Trim and crimp the edges, then fill and bake as directed.

While the pie is still hot, prepare the meringue. Preheat the oven to 350° F. Beat the egg whites, vanilla, and cream of tartar until the mixture holds stiff peaks. Gradually add the sugar, 1 tablespoon at a time, beating until very stiff and glossy. All the sugar must be dissolved. Spread the meringue over the pie filling, sealing it to the edge of the crust. Bake 12 to 15 minutes or until golden brown. Cool before serving.

NO. 28   # BANANA PIE

One 9-inch single-crust pie

Prebaked 9-inch pie shell
(Classic Single Crust or Graham Cracker Crust)

6 large bananas	½ teaspoon vanilla extract
1 cup heavy cream	1 ounce (1 square)
1 teaspoon confectioners' sugar	unsweetened baking chocolate, grated

Prepare the prebaked pie shell; cool completely.

Mash the bananas to a fine pulp. In a separate bowl, whip the cream until stiff peaks form. Beat in the confectioners' sugar and vanilla. Blend in the banana pulp. Turn the filling into the pie shell and sprinkle with grated chocolate. Chill until ready to serve.

NO. 29   # BLACKBERRY PIE

One 9-inch double-crust pie

Pastry for a 9-inch double-crust pie
(Classic Double Crust)

1 cup sugar	4 cups blackberries
⅓ cup flour	2 teaspoons lemon juice
1 teaspoon grated lemon zest	2 tablespoons unsalted butter or margarine
½ teaspoon mace	

Preheat the oven to 450° F. Prepare the pie pastry. Line the pie pan with the bottom crust, using half of the dough. Keep the remaining dough chilled.

Combine the sugar, flour, lemon zest, and mace. Add the blackberries and lemon juice. Mix well. Turn the filling into the crust and dot with butter. Roll out the top crust and lay it on the filling. Trim off any excess dough, crimp the edges, and prick with the tines of a fork to vent.

Bake at 450° F for 10 minutes. Reduce the heat to 350° F and bake about 30 minutes more or until golden brown.

NO. 30   BLUEBERRY MERINGUE PIE
One 9-inch single-crust pie

Recipe for Blackberry Pie (No. 29)

Meringue

3 large egg whites, at room
  temperature
½ teaspoon vanilla extract

¼ teaspoon cream of tartar
6 tablespoons superfine
  sugar

Prepare the recipe for Blackberry Pie, substituting the Classic Single Crust for the Classic Double Crust and replacing the blackberries with blueberries. Trim and crimp the edges, then bake as directed.

While the pie is still hot, prepare the meringue. Preheat the oven to 350° F. Beat the egg whites, vanilla, and cream of tartar until the mixture holds stiff peaks. Gradually add the sugar, 1 tablespoon at a time, beating until very stiff and glossy. All the sugar must be dissolved. Spread the meringue over the pie filling, sealing it to the edge of the crust. Bake 12 to 15 minutes or until golden brown. Cool before serving.

NO. 31   LATTICE-TOP BLUEBERRY PIE
One 9-inch lattice-top pie

Follow the recipe for Blackberry Pie (No. 29), making a lattice-top crust and using fresh blueberries for blackberries. After the pie is latticed and crimped, sprinkle 1 tablespoon of sugar over the lattice crust. Bake as directed.

NO. 32   **BLUEBERRY PECAN PIE**
                              One 9-inch double-crust pie

Pastry for a 9-inch double-crust pie
(Classic Double Crust)

½ cup sugar

¼ cup cornstarch

1 teaspoon grated orange
   zest

½ teaspoon nutmeg

¾ cup pecans, coarsely
   chopped

4 cups blueberries

2 tablespoons orange juice

2 tablespoons unsalted
   butter or margarine

Confectioners' sugar

Preheat the oven to 375° F. Prepare the pie pastry. Line the pie
pan with the bottom crust, using half of the dough. Keep the
remaining dough chilled.
   Combine the sugar, cornstarch, orange zest, nutmeg, and pecans.
Add the blueberries and orange juice. Mix well. Turn the filling
into the crust and dot with butter. Roll out the top crust and lay it
on the filling. Trim off any excess dough, crimp the edges, and
prick with the tines of a fork to vent. Bake 1 hour or until golden
brown. Sprinkle with confectioners' sugar when cooled.

NO. 33   **GLAZED BLUEBERRY PIE**
                              One 9-inch single-crust pie

Prebaked 9-inch pie shell
(Egg Crust)

8 ounces cream cheese, at
   room temperature

½ cup sour cream

⅓ cup dark brown sugar,
   firmly packed

½ teaspoon allspice

1 teaspoon cinnamon

4 cups blueberries

Glaze

⅓ cup sugar

2 tablespoons cornstarch

¾ cup unsweetened apple
   juice

1 tablespoon brandy

Prepare the prebaked pie shell; cool completely.
   Whip the cream cheese until smooth. Beat in the sour cream,
brown sugar, allspice, and cinnamon. Turn the filling into the pie

shell. Layer the blueberries over the filling.

To prepare the glaze, combine the sugar and cornstarch in a saucepan. Stir in the apple juice. Cook over moderate heat, stirring frequently, until the mixture is thick and clear. Stir in the brandy. Spoon the hot glaze over the blueberries. Chill until ready to serve.

NO. 34 # CANTALOUPE PIE

One 9-inch single-crust pie

Prebaked 9-inch pie shell
(Classic Single Crust or Graham Cracker Crust)

1 large cantaloupe melon	2 egg yolks, beaten
1 cup sugar	⅛ teaspoon ground ginger
2 tablespoons cornstarch	1 tablespoon lemon juice

Meringue

3 large egg whites, at room temperature	¼ teaspoon cream of tartar
½ teaspoon vanilla extract	6 tablespoons superfine sugar

Prepare the prebaked pie shell; cool completely.

Quarter and seed the cantaloupe, then remove the pulp from the rind. Reduce the melon pulp to a fine consistency in a food processor. Combine the sugar, and cornstarch in a saucepan. Stir in the melon pulp and cook over medium heat, stirring frequently, about 20 minutes or until thickened. Stir a small amount of the hot mixture into the egg yolks. Combine the egg yolk mixture with the mixture in the double boiler. Cook for 2 minutes more. Remove the pan from the heat. Stir in the ginger and the lemon juice. Turn the filling into the pie shell.

Preheat the oven to 350° F. While the filling is still hot, prepare the meringue. Beat the egg whites, vanilla, and cream of tartar until the mixture holds stiff peaks. Gradually add the sugar, 1 tablespoon at a time, beating until very stiff and glossy. All the sugar must be dissolved. Spread the meringue over the hot filling, sealing it to the edge of the crust. Bake 12 to 15 minutes or until golden brown. Cool, and chill until serving.

NO. 35   **CHERRY PIE**
One 9-inch double-crust pie

Pastry for a 9-inch double-crust pie
(Classic Double Crust)

⅓ cup sugar   1 tablespoon lemon juice
2 tablespoons cornstarch   ¼ teaspoon almond extract
4 cups pitted fresh sweet   2 tablespoons unsalted
  cherries   butter or margarine

Preheat the oven to 425° F. Prepare the pie pastry. Line the pie
pan with the bottom crust, using half of the dough. Keep the
remaining dough chilled.

Combine the sugar and cornstarch. Stir in the cherries, lemon
juice, and almond extract. Mix well. Turn the filling into the crust
and dot with butter. Roll out the top crust and lay it on the filling.
Trim off any excess dough, crimp the edges, and prick with the
tines of a fork to vent.

Bake at 425° F for 10 minutes. Reduce the heat to 375° F and
bake about 30 minutes more or until golden brown.

NO. 36   **DEEP-DISH CHERRY PIE**
One 9-inch single-crust pie

Pastry for a 9-inch single-crust pie
(Baking Powder Crust)

½ cup light brown sugar,   2 tablespoons lemon juice
  firmly packed   2 cups pitted fresh sweet
¼ cup cornstarch   cherries
1 teaspoon cinnamon   2 cups pitted fresh sour
¼ teaspoon nutmeg   cherries
2 cups cherry juice   2 tablespoons unsalted
                                           butter or margarine

Preheat the oven to 375° F. Prepare the pastry. Keep the dough
chilled until the filling is prepared.

Combine the sugar, cornstarch, cinnamon, and nutmeg in a
saucepan. Stir in the cherry juice and lemon juice. Cook over
medium heat, stirring constantly, until the mixture thickens. Remove the pan from the heat and stir in the cherries. Thoroughly
butter the bottom and sides of a 9-inch deep-dish pie pan. Turn
the filling into the pan and dot with butter. Roll out the pastry

and lay it on the filling. Trim off any excess dough, crimp the edges, and prick with the tines of a fork to vent.

Bake 35 minutes or until golden brown.

NO. 37   **DEEP-DISH BLUEBERRY PIE**

One 9-inch single-crust pie

Follow the recipe for Deep-Dish Cherry Pie (No. 36), substituting blueberries for cherries. Bake as directed.

NO. 38   **LATTICE-TOP SOUR CHERRY PIE**

One 9-inch lattice-top pie

Pastry for a 9-inch lattice-top pie
(Classic Double Crust)

1 cup plus 1 tablespoon sugar	4 cups pitted fresh sour cherries
3 tablespoons flour	¼ teaspoon almond extract
1 teaspoon cinnamon	2 tablespoons unsalted butter or margarine

Preheat the oven to 450° F. Prepare the pie pastry. Line the pie pan with the bottom crust, using half of the dough. Keep the remaining dough chilled.

Combine the sugar, flour, and cinnamon. Sprinkle one fourth of the sugar mixture evenly over the bottom of the crust. Stir the cherries and almond extract into the remaining sugar mixture. Turn the filling into the crust and dot with butter. Roll out, cut, and lay on the lattice strips. After the pie is latticed and crimped, sprinkle 1 tablespoon of sugar over the lattice crust.

Bake at 450° F for 10 minutes. Reduce the heat to 350° F and bake about 40 minutes more or until golden brown.

NO. 39   **OPEN-FACE CHERRY PIE**

One 9-inch single-crust,
decorated-top pie

Pastry for a 9-inch double-crust pie
(Classic Double Crust)

½ cup sugar	4 cups canned pitted sour
¼ cup flour	cherries, with juice
2 teaspoons uncooked	2 teaspoons lemon juice
tapioca	¼ teaspoon almond extract
¼ teaspoon nutmeg	2 tablespoons unsalted
	butter or margarine

Preheat the oven to 450° F. Prepare the pie pastry. Line the pie
pan with the bottom crust, using half of the dough. Keep the
remaining dough chilled.

Combine the sugar, flour, tapioca, and nutmeg. Mix well. Stir
in the cherries, lemon juice, and almond extract. Turn the filling
into the crust and dot with butter. Roll out the top crust and cut
out leaves from the pastry. Lay the pastry leaves around the pie
in a wreath pattern, with the points of the leaves facing to the
center.

Bake at 450° F for 10 minutes. Reduce the heat to 350° F and
bake about 25 minutes more or until golden brown.

NO. 40   **SOUR CHERRY PIE**

One 9-inch lattice-top pie

Pastry for a 9-inch lattice-top pie
(Classic Double Crust)

¾ cup light brown sugar,	¼ teaspoon almond extract
firmly packed	1 tablespoon Kirsch liqueur
5½ tablespoons uncooked	3 cups pitted fresh sour
tapioca	cherries
1¼ cups water	1 tablespoon sugar
1½ cups cherry juice	

Preheat the oven to 425° F. Prepare the pie pastry. Line the pie
pan with the bottom crust, using half of the dough. Keep the
remaining dough chilled.

Combine the brown sugar, tapioca, and ½ cup water. Mix until
smooth. Combine the cherry juice and the remaining ¾ cup of
the water in a saucepan. Bring to a boil and reduce the heat to

low. Stir in the sugar mixture. Cook over low heat, stirring frequently, until thickened. Remove the pan from the heat. Add the almond extract and the Kirsch, then stir in the cherries. Turn the filling into the crust. Roll out, cut, and lay on the lattice strips. After the pie is latticed and crimped, sprinkle 1 tablespoon of sugar over the lattice crust.

Bake at 425° F for 10 minutes. Reduce the heat to 375° F and bake about 30 minutes more or until golden brown.

CONCORD GRAPE PIE

NO. 41

One 9-inch double-crust pie

**Pastry for a 9-inch double-crust pie
(Classic Double Crust)**

4 cups Concord grapes
¾ cup sugar
3 tablespoons flour
1 tablespoon lemon juice

1 teaspoon grated lemon zest
2 tablespoons unsalted butter or margarine

Preheat the oven to 450° F. Prepare the pie pastry. Line the pie pan with the bottom crust, using half of the dough. Keep the remaining dough chilled.

Skin the grapes, reserving the skins. Place the grape pulp in a saucepan with no water. Cook, over medium heat, until the pulp comes to a boil. Remove the pan from the heat. Push the pulp through a strainer to remove the seeds. Combine the strained pulp with the reserved grape skins. Mix together the sugar and flour. Sprinkle one fourth of the sugar mixture evenly over the bottom of the crust. Add the grape mixture to the remaining sugar mixture and stir well. Add the lemon juice and the lemon zest. Turn the filling into the crust and dot with butter. Roll out the top crust and lay it on the filling. Trim off any excess dough, crimp the edges, and prick with the tines of a fork to vent.

Bake at 450° F for 10 minutes. Reduce the heat to 350° F and bake about 30 minutes more or until golden brown.

NO. 42   **OPEN-FACE CONCORD GRAPE PIE**

One 9-inch single-crust
decorated-top pie

Follow the recipe for Concord Grape Pie (No. 41), reserving the top crust for decoration. After the filling is turned into the crust, roll out the top crust and cut out leaves from the pastry, using a real grape leaf for a pattern. Lay the pastry leaves around the pie in a wreath pattern, with the points of the leaves facing to the center. Bake as directed.

NO. 43   **CRUMB-TOPPED CONCORD GRAPE PIE**

One 9-inch single-crust pie

Recipe for Concord Grape Pie (No. 41)

Crumb Topping

⅓ cup light brown sugar,   6 tablespoons unsalted
    firmly packed   butter or margarine
¾ cup flour   Sweetened whipped cream

Follow the recipe for Concord Grape Pie, substituting the Classic Single Crust for the Classic Double Crust. After the filling is turned into the crust, prepare the crumb topping. Mix together the brown sugar and flour. Using a pastry blender or the tines of a fork, cut in the butter until the mixture is crumbly. Sprinkle the crumbs evenly over the filled pie shell. Bake as directed. Serve with sweetened whipped cream.

NO. 44

CRANBERRY PIE

One 9-inch lattice-top pie

**Pastry for a 9-inch lattice-top pie
(Classic Double Crust)**

- 2 cups plus 1 tablespoon sugar
- 2 tablespoons flour
- 1 tablespoon grated orange zest
- ¼ teaspoon nutmeg

- 4 cups cranberries, coarsely chopped
- 3 tablespoons water
- 2 tablespoons unsalted butter or margarine

Preheat the oven to 450° F. Prepare the pie pastry. Line the pie pan with the bottom crust, using half of the dough. Keep the remaining dough chilled.

Combine 2 cups of the sugar, flour, orange zest, and nutmeg. Sprinkle one fourth of the sugar mixture evenly over the bottom of the crust. Stir the cranberries into the remaining sugar mixture. Turn the filling into the crust. Sprinkle on the water and dot with butter. Roll out, cut, and lay on the lattice strips. After the pie is latticed and crimped, sprinkle 1 tablespoon of sugar over the lattice crust.

Bake at 450° F for 10 minutes. Reduce the heat to 350° F and bake about 40 minutes more or until golden brown.

NO. 45

CRANBERRY MERINGUE PIE

One 9-inch single-crust pie

Recipe for Cranberry Pie (No. 44)

Meringue

- 3 large egg whites, at room temperature
- ½ teaspoon vanilla extract

- ¼ teaspoon cream of tartar
- 6 tablespoons superfine sugar

Prepare the recipe for Cranberry Pie, substituting the Classic Single Crust for the Classic Double Crust. Trim and crimp the edges, then bake as directed.

While the pie is still hot, prepare the meringue. Preheat the oven to 350° F. Beat the egg whites, vanilla, and cream of tartar until the mixture holds stiff peaks. Gradually add the sugar, 1 tablespoon at a time, beating until very stiff and glossy. All the sugar must be dissolved. Spread the meringue over the pie filling, sealing it to the edge of the crust. Bake 12 to 15 minutes or until golden brown. Cool before serving.

NO. 46   CAPE COD CRANBERRY PIE

One 9-inch "pie"

2 cups whole cranberries
1¼ cups sugar
½ cup walnuts, coarsely
   chopped
2 eggs, beaten
½ teaspoon vanilla extract

1 cup sifted flour
1¼ teaspoons baking powder
¾ cup unsalted butter or
   margarine, melted
Vanilla ice cream

Preheat the oven to 325° F. Thoroughly butter the bottom and sides of a 9-inch deep-dish pie pan.

Spread the cranberries evenly in the pie pan. Combine ¼ cup of the sugar with the walnuts. Sprinkle ½ cup of the sugar mixture over the cranberries. Beat the remaining 1 cup of sugar with the eggs and vanilla. Mix in the flour and baking powder. Stir in the melted butter. Pour the "crust" over the cranberries and top with the remaining sugar mixture.

Bake about 1 hour or until golden brown. Serve with vanilla ice cream.

NO. 47

GREEN CURRANT PIE
One 9-inch single-crust pie

Pastry for a 9-inch single-crust pie
(Classic Single Crust)
1½ cups sugar
2 tablespoons flour
½ teaspoon allspice
3½ cups mixed green and
    half-ripe currants

2 tablespoons unsalted
    butter or margarine
Baked pastry stars for
    decoration

Preheat the oven to 450° F. Prepare the pie pastry. Line the pie pan with the dough. Trim and crimp the edges.

Combine the sugar, flour, and allspice. Add the currants and mix well. Turn the filling into the crust and dot with butter.

Cover the pie with an inverted lightweight pie pan. Bake at 450° F for 10 minutes. Reduce the heat to 350° F and bake 10 minutes. Remove the covering and bake 15 to 20 minutes more. Decorate with baked pastry stars.

NO. 48

RED CURRANT PIE
One 9-inch single-crust pie

Pastry for a 9-inch single-crust pie
(Classic Single Crust)
3 tablespoons flour
1 cup sugar
2 egg yolks, beaten

2 tablespoons water
3 cups red currants

Meringue

3 large egg whites, at room
    temperature
½ teaspoon vanilla extract

¼ teaspoon cream of tartar
6 tablespoons superfine
    sugar

Preheat the oven to 450° F. Prepare the pie pastry. Line the pie pan with the dough. Trim and crimp the edges.

Combine the flour and sugar. Beat the egg yolks with the water and add to the flour mixture. Stir in the currants. Turn the filling into the crust.

Bake at 450° F for 10 minutes. Reduce the heat to 350° F. Cover with an inverted lightweight pie pan and bake 20 minutes. Remove the covering and bake 15 minutes more. Remove the pie from the oven and leave the oven on.

While the pie is still hot, prepare the meringue. Beat the egg whites, vanilla, and cream of tartar until the mixture holds stiff peaks. Gradually add the sugar, 1 tablespoon at a time, beating until very stiff and glossy. All the sugar must be dissolved. Spread the meringue over the pie filling, sealing it to the edge of the crust. Bake 12 to 15 minutes or until golden brown. Cool before serving.

NO. 49   **FRESH FIG PIE**

One 9-inch lattice-top pie

Pastry for a 9-inch lattice-top pie
(Classic Double Crust)

¾ cup light brown sugar, firmly packed

¼ teaspoon ground ginger

3 cups peeled, sliced fresh figs

3 tablespoons lemon juice

2 tablespoons unsalted butter or margarine

1 tablespoon sugar

Preheat the oven to 425° F. Prepare the pie pastry. Line the pie pan with the bottom crust, using half of the dough. Keep the remaining dough chilled.

Combine the brown sugar and ginger. Stir in the figs and lemon juice. Mix well. Turn the filling into the crust and dot with butter. Roll out, cut, and lay on the lattice strips. After the pie is latticed and crimped, sprinkle 1 tablespoon of sugar over the lattice crust.

Bake 30 minutes or until golden brown.

NO. 50   **GOOSEBERRY PIE**

One 9-inch double-crust pie

Pastry for a 9-inch double-crust pie
(Classic Double Crust)

1½ cups sugar

3 tablespoons flour

½ teaspoon cinnamon

3 cups gooseberries, stems and blossom ends removed

2 tablespoons unsalted butter or margarine

Preheat the oven to 450° F. Prepare the pie pastry. Line the pie pan with the bottom crust, using half of the dough. Keep the remaining dough chilled.

Combine the sugar, flour, and cinnamon. Sprinkle one fourth of the sugar mixture evenly over the bottom of the crust. Add the gooseberries to the remaining sugar mixture and mix well. Turn the filling into the crust and dot with butter. Roll out the top crust and lay it on the filling. Trim off any excess dough, crimp the edges, and prick with the tines of a fork to vent.

Bake at 450° F for 10 minutes. Reduce the heat to 350° F and bake 30 minutes more or until golden brown.

NO. 51   # OPEN-FACE GOOSEBERRY PIE

One 9-inch single-crust pie

Prebaked 9-inch pie shell
(Classic Single Crust or Graham Cracker Crust)

1½ cups sugar	2 cups gooseberries, stems
2 tablespoons uncooked	and blossom ends
tapioca	removed
½ cup orange juice	Sweetened whipped cream

Prepare the prebaked pie shell; cool completely.

Combine the sugar, tapioca, and orange juice in a saucepan. Cook over low heat, stirring frequently, until slightly thickened. Add the gooseberries. Continue to cook until the gooseberries are tender but not broken. Turn the filling into the pie shell. Cool, and serve with sweetened whipped cream.

NO. 52   # LATTICE-TOP LOGANBERRY PIE

One 9-inch lattice-top pie

Pastry for a 9-inch lattice-top pie
(Classic Double Crust)

1 cup plus 1 tablespoon	4 cups fresh loganberries
sugar	1 tablespoon lemon juice
5 tablespoons flour	2 tablespoons unsalted
½ teaspoon cinnamon	butter or margarine

Preheat the oven to 450° F. Prepare the pie pastry. Line the pie pan with the bottom crust, using half of the dough. Keep the remaining dough chilled.

Combine 1 cup sugar, flour, and cinnamon. Sprinkle one fourth of the sugar mixture evenly over the bottom of the crust. Add the loganberries and lemon juice to the remaining sugar mixture. Mix well. Turn the filling into the crust and dot with butter. Roll out, cut, and lay on the lattice strips. After the pie is latticed and crimped, sprinkle 1 tablespoon of sugar over the lattice crust.

Bake at 450° F for 10 minutes. Reduce the heat to 350° F and bake 35 to 45 minutes more or until golden brown.

NO. 53   **MANGO PIE**

One 9-inch double-crust pie

Pastry for a 9-inch double-crust pie
(Classic Double Crust)

4 cups peeled, thinly sliced ripe mangoes	⅛ teaspoon salt
½ cup water	2 tablespoons flour
1 cup dark brown sugar, firmly packed	

Hard Sauce

1 tablespoon unsalted butter or margarine	¼ cup dark brown sugar, firmly packed

Preheat the oven to 450° F. Prepare the pie pastry. Line the pie pan with the bottom crust, using half of the dough. Keep the remaining dough chilled.

Combine the mangoes and water in a large saucepan. Cook over medium heat, stirring frequently, for 20 minutes. Drain any remaining liquid from the mangoes and set aside. Combine 1 cup of the brown sugar, salt, and flour. Sprinkle one fourth of the sugar mixture evenly over the bottom of the crust. Spoon the mangoes into the crust and top with the remaining sugar mixture. Roll out the top crust and lay it on the filling. Trim off any excess dough, crimp the edges, and prick with the tines of a fork to vent.

Bake at 450° F for 10 minutes. Reduce the heat to 350° F and bake 25 to 30 minutes more or until golden brown. Serve with hard sauce, prepared by stirring the butter and ¼ cup of brown sugar together over low heat, until liquid.

NO. 54   # NECTARINE PIE

One 9-inch lattice-top pie

Pastry for a 9-inch lattice-top pie (Classic Double Crust)

½ cup plus 1 tablespoon sugar

2 tablespoons flour

¼ teaspoon nutmeg

1 egg, beaten

½ cup heavy cream

4 cups peeled, thinly sliced nectarines

Preheat the oven to 450° F. Prepare the pie pastry. Line the pie pan with the bottom crust, using half of the dough. Keep the remaining dough chilled.

Combine ½ cup of the sugar, flour, and nutmeg. Add the egg and cream and mix well. Stir in the nectarines. Turn the filling into the crust and dot with butter. Roll out, cut, and lay on the lattice strips. After the pie is latticed and crimped, sprinkle 1 tablespoon of sugar over the lattice crust.

Bake at 450° F for 10 minutes. Reduce the heat to 350° F and bake 30 to 35 minutes more or until golden brown.

NO. 55   # DEEP-DISH PEACH PIE

One 9-inch single-crust pie

Pastry for a 9-inch single-crust pie (Baking Powder Crust)

4 cups peeled, thinly sliced peaches

1 teaspoon cornstarch

½ teaspoon grated lemon zest

½ cup light brown sugar, firmly packed

½ teaspoon ground ginger

1 tablespoon water

2 tablespoons lemon juice

2 tablespoons unsalted butter or margarine

Sweetened whipped cream

Preheat the oven to 400° F. Prepare the pastry. Keep the dough chilled until the filling is prepared.

Thoroughly butter the bottom and sides of a 9-inch deep-dish pie pan. Arrange the peaches in the pan. Sprinkle on the cornstarch and lemon zest. In a saucepan, combine the sugar, ginger, water, and lemon juice. Bring the mixture to a boil while stirring. Pour the hot mixture over the peaches and dot with butter. Roll out the dough and lay it on the filling. Trim off any excess dough, crimp the edges, and prick with the tines of a fork to vent.

Bake 25 to 30 minutes or until golden brown. Serve warm, with sweetened whipped cream.

NO. 56   **DEEP-DISH PEAR PIE**
One 9-inch single-crust pie

Follow the recipe for Deep-Dish Peach Pie (No. 55), substituting peeled, cored, and sliced Bosc pears for peaches. Bake as directed.

NO. 57   **PEACH PIE**
One 9-inch double-crust pie

**Pastry for a 9-inch double-crust pie
(Classic Double Crust)**

½ cup sugar	5 cups peeled, sliced
2 tablespoons cornstarch	peaches
½ teaspoon cinnamon	1 tablespoon lemon juice
¼ teaspoon nutmeg	2 tablespoons unsalted
	butter or margarine

Preheat the oven to 425° F. Prepare the pie pastry. Line the pie pan with the bottom crust, using half of the dough. Keep the remaining dough chilled.

Combine the sugar, cornstarch, cinnamon, and nutmeg. Add the peaches and lemon juice and mix well. Turn the filling into the crust and dot with butter. Roll out the top crust and lay it on the filling. Trim off any excess dough, crimp the edges, and prick with the tines of a fork to vent.

Bake 40 minutes or until golden brown.

NO. 58   **PEAR PIE**
One 9-inch double-crust pie

Follow the recipe for Peach Pie (No. 57), substituting peeled, cored, and sliced Bosc pears for peaches. Bake as directed.

NO. 59   **LATTICE-TOP PEACH PIE**

One 9-inch lattice-top pie

Follow the recipe for Peach Pie (No. 57), making a lattice-top crust. After the pie is latticed and crimped, sprinkle 1 tablespoon of sugar over the lattice crust. Bake as directed.

NO. 60   **LATTICE-TOP PEAR PIE**

One 9-inch lattice-top pie

Follow the recipe for Peach Pie (No. 57), making a lattice-top crust and using peeled, cored, and sliced Bosc pears in place of peaches. After the pie is latticed and crimped, sprinkle 1 tablespoon of sugar over the lattice crust. Bake as directed.

NO. 61   **OPEN-FACE PEACH PIE**

One 9-inch single-crust pie

Pastry for a 9-inch single-crust pie (Classic Single Crust)

½ cup sugar	1 cup heavy cream
2 tablespoons cornstarch	Sweetened whipped cream
10 large peaches, peeled and halved	

Preheat the oven to 450° F. Prepare the pie pastry. Line the pie pan with the dough. Trim and crimp the edges.

Mix together the sugar and the cornstarch. Press three-fourths of the sugar mixture into the bottom and up the sides of the crust. Arrange the peach halves, cut side up, in concentric circles in the crust. Sprinkle the peaches with the remaining sugar mixture. Pour the cream over the peaches, filling each peach center.

Bake at 450° F for 10 minutes. Reduce the heat to 325° F and cover with an inverted lightweight pie pan. Bake 20 minutes. Remove the cover and bake 15 minutes more. Serve warm, with sweetened whipped cream.

NO. 62   **PEACH MERINGUE PIE**
                          One 9-inch single-crust pie

Recipe for Open-Face Peach Pie (No. 61)

Meringue

3 large egg whites, at room   ¼ teaspoon cream of tartar
   temperature   6 tablespoons superfine
½ teaspoon vanilla extract   sugar

Follow the recipe for Open-Face Peach Pie.

While the pie is still hot, prepare the meringue. Preheat the oven to 350° F. Beat the egg whites, vanilla, and cream of tartar until the mixture holds stiff peaks. Gradually add the sugar, 1 tablespoon at a time, beating until very stiff and glossy. All the sugar must be dissolved. Spread the meringue over the pie filling, sealing it to the edge of the crust. Bake 12 to 15 minutes or until golden brown. Cool before serving.

NO. 63   **OPEN-FACE PEAR PIE**
                          One 9-inch single-crust pie

Pastry for a 9-inch single-crust pie
(Classic Single Crust)

¼ cup flour   ½ teaspoon allspice
⅔ cup light brown sugar,   5 cups peeled, cored, and
   firmly packed   thinly sliced Bartlett
1 cup heavy cream   pears
1 tablespoon lemon juice   Cinnamon sugar
1 teaspoon grated lemon
   zest

Preheat the oven to 400° F. Prepare the pie pastry. Line the pie pan with the dough. Trim and crimp the edges.

Combine the flour and sugar. Stir in the cream, lemon juice, lemon zest, and allspice. Add the pears and mix well. Turn the filling into the crust. Sprinkle the top of the pie with cinnamon sugar.

Bake 45 to 50 minutes or until golden brown.

NO. 64   **PEAR CRUMB PIE**

One 9-inch single-crust pie

Pastry for a 9-inch single-crust pie
(Classic Single Crust)

½ cup sugar

¾ cup plus 2 tablespoons
  flour

2 teaspoons grated lemon
  zest

½ teaspoon nutmeg

5 cups peeled, cored, and
  thinly sliced Bartlett
  pears

3 tablespoons lemon juice

⅓ cup light brown sugar,
  firmly packed

6 tablespoons unsalted
  butter or margarine

Sweetened whipped cream

Preheat the oven to 400° F. Prepare the pie pastry. Line the pie pan with the dough. Trim and crimp the edges.

Combine the sugar, 2 tablespoons of flour, lemon zest, and nutmeg. Add the pears and lemon juice and mix well. Turn the filling into the crust. In another bowl, mix together the brown sugar and ¾ cup of flour. Using a pastry blender or the tines of a fork, cut in the butter until the mixture is crumbly. Sprinkle the crumbs evenly over the filling.

Bake 40 to 45 minutes or until golden brown. Serve with sweetened whipped cream.

NO. 65   **LATTICE-TOP PLUM PIE**

One 9-inch lattice-top pie

Pastry for a 9-inch lattice-top pie
(Classic Double Crust)

½ cup plus 1 tablespoon
  sugar

¼ cup flour

½ teaspoon allspice

1 teaspoon grated orange
  zest

4 cups peeled, sliced plums

1 tablespoon orange juice

2 tablespoons unsalted
  butter or margarine

Confectioners' sugar

Preheat the oven to 450° F. Prepare the pie pastry. Line the pie pan with the bottom crust, using half of the dough. Keep the remaining dough chilled.

Combine the sugar, flour, allspice, and orange zest. Add the plums and orange juice and mix well. Turn the filling into the crust and dot with butter. Roll out, cut, and lay on the lattice strips. After the pie is latticed and crimped, sprinkle 1 tablespoon of sugar over the lattice crust.

Bake at 450° F for 10 minutes. Reduce the heat to 350° F and bake about 30 minutes more or until golden brown. Sprinkle with confectioners' sugar while still warm.

NO. 66   **PINEAPPLE MERINGUE PIE**

One 9-inch single-crust pie

Prebaked 9-inch pie shell
(Classic Single Crust or Graham Cracker Crust)

2 tablespoons cornstarch	1 tablespoon unsalted butter
2 tablespoons sugar	or margarine
2 cups canned crushed	1 tablespoon lemon juice
pineapple, drained	1 tablespoon grated lemon
	zest

Meringue

3 large egg whites, at room	¼ teaspoon cream of tartar
temperature	6 tablespoons superfine
½ teaspoon vanilla extract	sugar

Prepare the prebaked pie shell; cool completely.

In the top of a double boiler, combine the cornstarch, sugar, and pineapple. Set over simmering water and cook, stirring frequently, for 20 minutes or until the mixture has thickened. Remove the pan from the heat. Stir in the butter, lemon juice, and lemon zest. Cool the filling, then pour it into the pie shell.

Preheat the oven to 350° F. To prepare the meringue, beat the egg whites, vanilla, and cream of tartar until the mixture holds stiff peaks. Gradually add the sugar, 1 tablespoon at a time, beating until very stiff and glossy. All the sugar must be dissolved. Spread the meringue over the filling, sealing it to the edge of the crust. Bake 12 to 15 minutes or until golden brown. Cool before serving.

NO. 67   **PRUNE PIE**

One 9-inch double-crust pie

**Pastry for a 9-inch double-crust pie
(Classic Double Crust)**

16 ounces dried pitted prunes	**2 tablespoons unsalted**
⅓ cup sugar	**butter or margarine**
2 tablespoons flour	**1 tablespoon lemon juice**

Place the prunes in a saucepan and cover with cold water. Let the mixture soak overnight. The next day, bring the mixture to a boil, then reduce the heat to low and simmer for 10 minutes. Remove the pan from the heat. Drain the prunes and set aside.

Preheat the oven to 450° F. Prepare the pie pastry. Line the pie pan with the bottom crust, using half of the dough. Keep the remaining dough chilled.

Combine the sugar and flour in a saucepan. Stir in the prunes. Simmer for 10 minutes. Remove the pan from the heat. Stir in the butter and lemon juice. Let the filling cool, then pour it into the crust. Roll out the top crust and lay it on the filling. Trim off any excess dough, crimp the edges, and prick with the tines of a fork to vent.

Bake at 450° F for 10 minutes. Reduce the heat to 350° F and bake 25 minutes more or until golden brown.

NO. 68   **DRIED APRICOT PIE**

One 9-inch double-crust pie

Follow the recipe for Prune Pie (No. 67), substituting dried apricot halves for prunes. Bake as directed.

NO. 69   **FLUFFY PRUNE PIE**
                                   One 9-inch single-crust pie

Prebaked 9-inch pie shell
(Classic Single Crust or Graham Cracker Crust)
16 ounces dried pitted prunes   1 teaspoon lemon juice
 ¾ cup sugar   2 egg whites
 ¾ cup walnuts, coarsely   Sweetened whipped cream
     chopped
 1 teaspoon grated lemon
     zest

Place the prunes in a mixing bowl and cover with cold water. Let
the mixture soak overnight. The next day, drain the prunes and
cut into small pieces.
    Prepare the prebaked pie shell; cool completely.
    Preheat the oven to 325° F. Combine the prunes with the sugar,
walnuts, lemon zest, and lemon juice. In a separate bowl, beat the
egg whites until they form stiff peaks. Fold the egg whites into
the prune mixture. Turn the filling into the pie shell.
    Bake 30 minutes. Serve cool, with sweetened whipped cream.

NO. 70   **RAISIN PIE**
                                   One 9-inch single-crust pie

Pastry for a 9-inch single-crust pie
(Classic Single Crust)
 3 eggs   2 tablespoons unsalted
 1 cup light brown sugar,   butter or margarine,
     firmly packed   melted
 1 teaspoon cinnamon   1 cup raisins
 ¼ teaspoon nutmeg   ½ cup walnuts, coarsely
 ⅛ teaspoon ground ginger   chopped
 2½ teaspoons orange juice
 1 teaspoon grated lemon
     zest

Preheat the oven to 375° F. Prepare the pie pastry. Line the pie
pan with the dough. Trim and crimp the edges.
    Beat the eggs until light and foamy. Beat the sugar, cinnamon,
nutmeg, ginger, orange juice, lemon zest, and butter. Stir in the
raisins and walnuts. Turn the filling into the crust.
    Bake 40 minutes or until the center of the pie is set.

NO. 71 LATTICE-TOP RAISIN PIE

One 9-inch lattice-top pie

Pastry for a 9-inch lattice-top pie
(Classic Double Crust)

1 cup dark brown sugar,
  firmly packed
3 tablespoons cornstarch
2 cups golden raisins
1 cup water
¾ cup orange juice
¼ cup lemon juice

1 teaspoon grated orange
  zest
1 teaspoon grated lemon
  zest
1 teaspoon cinnamon
½ cup pecans, coarsely
  chopped
1 tablespoon sugar

Preheat the oven to 400° F. Prepare the pie pastry. Line the pie pan with the bottom crust, using half of the dough. Keep the remaining dough chilled.

Combine the brown sugar and cornstarch in a large saucepan. Add the raisins, water, orange juice, lemon juice, orange zest, lemon zest, and cinnamon. Mix well. Cook, over medium heat, stirring constantly, until the mixture thickens. Remove the pan from the heat. Stir in the pecans. Let the filling cool, then turn it into the crust. Roll out, cut, and lay on the lattice strips. After the pie is latticed and crimped, sprinkle 1 tablespoon of sugar over the lattice crust.

Bake 30 to 35 minutes or until golden brown.

NO. 72 RASPBERRY PIE

One 9-inch double-crust pie

Pastry for a 9-inch double-crust pie
(Classic Double Crust)

4 cups raspberries
½ cup water
1 tablespoon unsalted butter
  or margarine
1 cup light brown sugar,
  firmly packed

1 tablespoon lemon juice
½ teaspoon cinnamon
½ teaspoon allspice

Preheat the oven to 450° F. Prepare the pie pastry. Line the pie pan with the bottom crust, using half of the dough. Keep the remaining dough chilled.

Combine the raspberries, water, butter, and sugar in a large saucepan. Cook over low heat, stirring frequently, for 5 minutes. Remove the pan from the heat. Stir in the lemon juice, cinnamon, and allspice. Let the filling cool, then turn it into the crust. Roll out the top crust and lay it on the filling. Trim off any excess dough, crimp the edges, and prick with the tines of a fork to vent.

Bake at 450° F for 10 minutes. Reduce the heat to 350° F and bake 30 minutes more or until golden brown.

NO. 73   **RASPBERRY MERINGUE PIE**
                              One 9-inch single-crust pie

Recipe for Raspberry Pie (No. 72)

Meringue

  3 large egg whites, at room   ¼ teaspoon cream of tartar
    temperature   6 tablespoons superfine
  ½ teaspoon vanilla extract   sugar

Prepare the recipe for Raspberry Pie, substituting the Classic Single Crust for the Classic Double Crust. Trim and crimp the edges, then fill and bake as directed.

While the pie is still hot, prepare the meringue. Preheat the oven to 350° F. Beat the egg whites, vanilla, and cream of tartar until the mixture holds stiff peaks. Gradually add the sugar, 1 tablespoon at a time, beating until very stiff and glossy. All the sugar must be dissolved. Spread the meringue over the pie filling, sealing it to the edge of the crust. Bake 12 to 15 minutes or until golden brown. Cool before serving.

NO. 74   **STRAWBERRY PIE**
                              One 9-inch double-crust pie

Follow the recipe for Raspberry Pie (No. 72), substituting sliced fresh strawberries for raspberries. Bake as directed.

NO. 75   **STRAWBERRY MERINGUE PIE**

One 9-inch single-crust pie

Recipe for Raspberry Pie (No. 72)

Meringue

3 large egg whites, at room temperature
½ teaspoon vanilla extract

¼ teaspoon cream of tartar
6 tablespoons superfine sugar

Prepare the recipe for Raspberry Pie, substituting the Classic Single Crust for the Classic Double Crust and using sliced fresh strawberries in place of raspberries. Trim and crimp the edges, then fill and bake as directed.

While the pie is still hot, prepare the meringue. Preheat the oven to 350° F. Beat the egg whites, vanilla, and cream of tartar until the mixture holds stiff peaks. Gradually add the sugar, 1 tablespoon at a time, beating until very stiff and glossy. All the sugar must be dissolved. Spread the meringue over the pie filling, sealing it to the edge of the crust. Bake 12 to 15 minutes or until golden brown. Cool before serving.

NO. 76   **LATTICE-TOP RASPBERRY PIE**

One 9-inch lattice-top pie

Pastry for a 9-inch lattice-top pie (Classic Double Crust)

½ cup plus 1 tablespoon sugar
½ cup flour
½ teaspoon allspice

4 cups fresh raspberries
½ teaspoon lemon juice
2 tablespoons unsalted butter or margarine

Preheat the oven to 450° F. Prepare the pie pastry. Line the pie pan with the bottom crust, using half of the dough. Keep the remaining dough chilled.

Combine ½ cup of the sugar, flour, and allspice. Add the raspberries and lemon juice and mix well. Turn the filling into the crust and dot with butter. Roll out, cut, and lay on the lattice strips. After the pie is latticed and crimped, sprinkle 1 tablespoon of sugar over the lattice crust.

Bake at 450° F for 10 minutes. Reduce the heat to 350° F and bake 30 minutes more or until golden brown.

NO. 77   **LATTICE-TOP STRAWBERRY PIE**
                                    One 9-inch lattice-top pie

Follow the recipe for Lattice-Top Raspberry Pie (No. 76), substituting sliced fresh strawberries for raspberries. Bake as directed.

NO. 78   **RASPBERRY SOUR CREAM PIE**
                                    One 9-inch single-crust pie

Pastry for a 9-inch single-crust pie
(Classic Single Crust)

2 tablespoons flour	3 tablespoons dark brown
4 cups raspberries	sugar, firmly packed
1 cup sour cream	½ teaspoon cinnamon
	1 teaspoon lemon juice

Preheat the oven to 375° F. Prepare the pie pastry. Line the pie pan with the dough. Trim and crimp the edges.

Sprinkle the flour in the bottom of the crust. Arrange the raspberries on top of the flour. Spread the sour cream over the raspberries. Combine the sugar with the cinnamon and lemon juice. Sprinkle the mixture over the top of the filling.

Bake 35 to 40 minutes.

NO. 79   **BLACKBERRY SOUR CREAM PIE**
                                    One 9-inch single-crust pie

Follow the recipe for Raspberry Sour Cream Pie (No. 78), substituting blackberries for raspberries. Bake as directed.

NO. 80   **BLUEBERRY SOUR CREAM PIE**
                                    One 9-inch single-crust pie

Follow the recipe for Raspberry Sour Cream Pie (No. 78), substituting blueberries for raspberries. Bake as directed.

NO. 81 **PEACH SOUR CREAM PIE**
One 9-inch single-crust pie

Follow the recipe for Raspberry Sour Cream Pie (No. 78), substituting peeled, sliced peaches for raspberries. Bake as directed.

NO. 82 **STRAWBERRY SOUR CREAM PIE**
One 9-inch single-crust pie

Follow the recipe for Raspberry Sour Cream Pie (No. 78), substituting sliced fresh strawberries for raspberries. Bake as directed.

NO. 83 **RHUBARB PIE**
One 9-inch double-crust pie

Pastry for a 9-inch double-crust pie (Classic Double Crust)

1 cup sugar	4 cups diced fresh rhubarb
3 tablespoons flour	1 teaspoon lemon juice
½ teaspoon cinnamon	2 tablespoons unsalted butter or margarine

Preheat the oven to 450° F. Prepare the pie pastry. Line the pie pan with the bottom crust, using half of the dough. Keep the remaining dough chilled.

Mix together the sugar, flour, and cinnamon. Add the rhubarb and lemon juice. Mix well. Turn the filling into the crust and dot with butter. Roll out the top crust and lay it on the filling. Trim off any excess dough, crimp the edges, and prick with the tines of a fork to vent.

Bake at 450° F for 10 minutes. Reduce the heat to 350° F and bake 25 to 30 minutes more or until golden brown.

NO. 84   **RHUBARB MERINGUE PIE**

One 9-inch single-crust pie

Recipe for Rhubarb Pie (No. 83)

Meringue

3 large egg whites, at room
   temperature
½ teaspoon vanilla extract

¼ teaspoon cream of tartar
6 tablespoons superfine
   sugar

Prepare the recipe for Rhubarb Pie, substituting the Classic Single
Crust for the Classic Double Crust. Trim and crimp the edges,
then fill and bake as directed.

While the pie is still hot, prepare the meringue. Preheat the
oven to 350° F. Beat the egg whites, vanilla, and cream of tartar
until the mixture holds stiff peaks. Gradually add the sugar, 1
tablespoon at a time, beating until very stiff and glossy. All the
sugar must be dissolved. Spread the meringue over the pie filling,
sealing it to the edge of the crust. Bake 12 to 15 minutes or until
golden brown. Cool before serving.

NO. 85   **DEEP-DISH RHUBARB PIE**

One 9-inch single-crust pie

**Pastry for a 9-inch single-crust pie
(Baking Powder Crust)**

1 cup dark brown sugar,
   firmly packed
3 tablespoons flour
¼ teaspoon salt
1 teaspoon grated lemon
   zest

4 cups diced fresh rhubarb
3 tablespoons unsalted
   butter or margarine,
   melted
Vanilla ice cream

Preheat the oven to 450° F. Prepare the pastry. Keep the dough
chilled until the filling is prepared.

Combine the sugar, flour, salt, and lemon zest. Add the rhubarb
and butter and mix well. Thoroughly butter the bottom and sides
of a 9-inch deep-dish pie pan. Turn the filling into the pan. Roll
out the pastry and lay it on the filling. Trim off any excess dough,
crimp the edges, and prick with the tines of a fork to vent.

Bake at 450° F for 10 minutes. Reduce the heat to 350° F and
bake about 30 minutes more or until golden brown. Serve warm,
with vanilla ice cream.

NO. 86 **RHUBARB SOUFFLÉ PIE**

One 9-inch single-crust pie

**Pastry for a 9-inch single-crust pie
(Classic Single Crust)**

1¼ cups sugar
½ teaspoon cinnamon
⅛ teaspoon ground ginger
2 tablespoons flour
1¾ cups unsweetened rhubarb
    puree
½ cup canned crushed
    pineapple, drained

1 tablespoon chopped
    candied orange peel
2 eggs, separated
2 tablespoons unsalted
    butter or margarine,
    melted

Preheat the oven to 450° F. Prepare the pie pastry. Line the pie pan with the dough. Trim and crimp the edges.

Mix together the sugar, cinnamon, ginger, and flour. Stir in the rhubarb puree, pineapple, and orange peel. Mix well. Beat the egg yolks. Add the egg yolks and melted butter to the rhubarb mixture. Beat the egg whites until they form stiff peaks. Fold the egg whites into the mixture. Turn the filling into the crust.

Bake at 450° F for 10 minutes. Reduce the heat to 350° F and bake 35 minutes more.

NO. 87 **SPICY RHUBARB CRUMB PIE**

One 9-inch single-crust pie

**Pastry for a 9-inch single-crust pie
(Classic Single Crust)**

1 cup sugar
⅓ cup cornstarch
1 teaspoon cinnamon
¼ teaspoon nutmeg
¼ teaspoon ground cloves
4 cups diced fresh rhubarb

¾ cup water
1 tablespoon lemon juice
½ cup quick-cooking oats
2 tablespoons light brown
    sugar, firmly packed
¼ cup unsalted butter or
    margarine, melted

Preheat the oven to 425° F. Prepare the pie pastry. Line the pie pan with the dough. Trim and crimp the edges.

In a saucepan, combine the sugar, cornstarch, cinnamon, nutmeg, and cloves. Add the rhubarb, water, and lemon juice. Mix well. Cook over low heat, stirring frequently, for about 10 minutes or until the mixture thickens. Remove the pan from the heat. Turn the filling into the crust. Mix together the oats and butter. Sprinkle the oat mixture evenly over the top of the pie.

Bake 25 minutes or until golden brown.

Combination Fruit Pies

Sun-sweetened strawberries, delicately freckled apricots, rosy-cheeked apples, and elegant pears are all the basis for many marvelous pies. Combination fruit pies mix and match complementary ingredients, with results often more delicious than many of their single-fruit cousins. The pies presented in this chapter offer classic fruit combinations as well as a number of tempting creations from the myriad possibilities of nature's sweetest harvest. You'll find that once the basic recipe for a combination fruit pie is mastered, ideas for many other combination pies easily come to mind.

APRICOT PRUNE LATTICE-TOP PIE

One 9-inch lattice-top pie

Pastry for a 9-inch lattice-top pie
(Classic Double Crust)

2 cups coarsely chopped dried apricots	2 tablespoons cornstarch
½ cup coarsely chopped dried pitted prunes	2 tablespoons lemon juice
1 cup water	2 teaspoons grated lemon zest
½ cup orange juice	2 tablespoons dry sherry
½ cup light brown sugar, firmly packed	1 tablespoon sugar
	¼ cup pecans, coarsely chopped

Preheat the oven to 425° F. Prepare the pie pastry. Line the pie pan with the bottom crust, using half of the dough. Keep the remaining dough chilled.

In a large saucepan, combine the apricots, prunes, water, and orange juice. Bring the mixture to a boil and reduce the heat to low. Cook, stirring frequently, for 5 minutes. Combine the brown sugar and cornstarch and stir into the fruit mixture. Cook for 3 minutes more. Remove the pan from the heat. Stir in the lemon juice, lemon zest, and sherry. Turn the filling into the crust. Roll out, cut, and lay on the lattice strips. After the pie is latticed and crimped, sprinkle the sugar and pecans over the lattice crust.

Bake 35 minutes or until golden brown.

BLUEBERRY CHERRY PIE

One 9-inch double-crust pie

Pastry for a 9-inch double-crust pie
(Classic Double Crust)

½ cup sugar	2 cups blueberries
⅓ cup flour	2 cups fresh sweet cherries, pitted and halved
1 teaspoon grated lemon zest	2 teaspoons lemon juice
½ teaspoon mace	2 tablespoons unsalted butter or margarine

Preheat the oven to 450° F. Prepare the pie pastry. Line the pie pan with the bottom crust, using half of the dough. Keep the remaining dough chilled.

Combine the sugar, flour, lemon zest, and mace. Add the blue-

berries, cherries, and lemon juice. Mix well. Turn the filling into
the crust and dot with butter. Roll out the top crust and lay it on
the filling. Trim off any excess dough, crimp the edges, and prick
with the tines of a fork to vent.

Bake at 450° F for 10 minutes. Reduce the heat to 350° F and
bake 30 minutes more or until golden brown.

NO. 90   **RASPBERRY CHERRY PIE**
One 9-inch double-crust pie

Follow the recipe for Blueberry Cherry Pie (No. 89), substituting
raspberries for blueberries. Bake as directed.

NO. 91   **BLUEBERRY RED CURRANT PIE**
One 9-inch double-crust pie

Follow the recipe for Blueberry Cherry Pie (No. 89), using 3 cups
of blueberries and 1 cup of red currants. Bake as directed.

NO. 92   **CRANBERRY ORANGE PIE**
One 9-inch single-crust pie

**Pastry for a 9-inch single-crust pie
(Classic Single Crust)**

4 cups cranberries, finely chopped	1½ cups sugar
¾ cup orange juice	2 tablespoons unsalted butter or margarine, melted
1 teaspoon grated orange zest	3½ teaspoons uncooked tapioca

Preheat the oven to 450° F. Prepare the pie pastry. Line the pie
pan with the dough. Trim and crimp the edges.

Combine the cranberries, orange juice, orange zest, sugar, butter,
and tapioca. Mix well. Turn the filling into the crust.

Bake at 450° F for 10 minutes. Reduce the heat to 350° F and
bake 35 minutes more or until golden brown.

NO. 93

CRANBERRY RAISIN LATTICE-TOP PIE

One 9-inch lattice-top pie

Pastry for a 9-inch lattice-top pie
(Classic Double Crust)

¾ cup light brown sugar,
  firmly packed
½ cup water
2 cups cranberries
1 cup raisins, coarsely
  chopped

1 tablespoon uncooked
  tapioca
½ cup orange juice
2 tablespoons unsalted
  butter or margarine
1 tablespoon sugar

Preheat the oven to 450° F. Prepare the pie pastry. Line the pie pan with the bottom crust, using half of the dough. Keep the remaining dough chilled.

Combine the brown sugar and water in a large saucepan. Bring the mixture to a boil and add the cranberries. Cook, stirring frequently, for 5 minutes. Remove the pan from the heat and let stand for 5 minutes. Add the raisins and cook 5 minutes more. Remove the pan from the heat. Stir in the tapioca and orange juice. If the mixture is very juicy, pour off some of the excess liquid. Turn the filling into the crust and dot with butter. Roll out, cut, and lay on the lattice strips. After the pie is latticed and crimped, sprinkle 1 tablespoon of sugar over the lattice crust.

Bake at 450° F for 10 minutes. Reduce the heat to 350° F and bake 35 minutes more or until golden brown.

NO. 94

ELDERBERRY GRAPE PIE

One 9-inch double-crust pie

Pastry for a 9-inch double-crust pie
(Classic Double Crust)

2 tablespoons flour
½ cup light brown sugar,
  firmly packed
1 teaspoon cinnamon
3 cups elderberries

¼ cup green seedless grapes
2 tablespoons unsalted
  butter or margarine
1 tablespoon cider vinegar

Preheat the oven to 450° F. Prepare the pie pastry. Line the pie pan with the bottom crust, using half of the dough. Keep the remaining dough chilled.

Combine the flour, sugar, and cinnamon. Sprinkle one fourth of the flour mixture evenly over the bottom of the crust. Add the elderberries and grapes to the remaining flour mixture. Mix well. Turn the filling into the crust and dot with butter. Sprinkle the vinegar over the top of the pie. Roll out the top crust and lay it on the filling. Trim off any excess dough, crimp the edges, and prick with the tines of a fork to vent.

Bake at 450° F for 10 minutes. Reduce the heat to 350° F and bake 35 to 40 minutes more or until golden brown.

NO. 95   **GRAPE RASPBERRY PIE**

One 9-inch lattice-top pie

Pastry for a 9-inch lattice-top pie
(Classic Double Crust)

2 cups seedless green grapes	½ cup plus 1 tablespoon
2 cups raspberries	sugar
1 teaspoon lemon juice	2 tablespoons flour

Preheat the oven to 450° F. Prepare the pie pastry. Line the pie pan with the bottom crust, using half of the dough. Keep the remaining dough chilled.

Crush the grapes slightly to break the skins. Mix the grapes with the raspberries and lemon juice. Combine the sugar and the flour. Sprinkle one fourth of the sugar mixture over the bottom of the crust. Stir the remaining sugar mixture into the fruit. Turn the filling into the crust. Roll out, cut, and lay on the lattice strips. After the pie is latticed and crimped, sprinkle 1 tablespoon of sugar over the lattice crust.

Bake at 450° F for 10 minutes. Reduce the heat to 350° F and bake about 35 minutes more or until golden brown.

NO. 96   # LEMON RAISIN PIE
One 9-inch double-crust pie

Pastry for a 9-inch double-crust pie
(Classic Double Crust)

1 cup raisins, coarsely chopped	1 tablespoon flour
Juice and grated zest of one large lemon	2 tablespoons unsalted butter or margarine
1 cup cold water	

Preheat the oven to 450° F. Prepare the pie pastry. Line the pie pan with the bottom crust, using half of the dough. Keep the remaining dough chilled.

Combine the raisins, lemon juice, lemon zest, water, and flour. Mix well. Turn the filling into the crust and dot with butter. Roll out the top crust and lay it on the filling. Trim off any excess dough, crimp the edges, and prick with the tines of a fork to vent.

Bake at 450° F for 10 minutes. Reduce the heat to 350° F and bake 35 to 40 minutes more or until golden brown.

NO. 97   # PEACH CHERRY PIE
One 9-inch lattice-top pie

Pastry for a 9-inch lattice-top pie
(Classic Double Crust)

½ cup plus 1 tablespoon sugar	¼ teaspoon almond extract
2 tablespoons flour	1 tablespoon lemon juice
2 cups peeled, sliced peaches	2 tablespoons unsalted butter or margarine
2 cups halved, pitted fresh sweet cherries	

Preheat the oven to 400° F. Prepare the pie pastry. Line the pie pan with the bottom crust, using half of the dough. Keep the remaining dough chilled.

Mix together ½ cup sugar and the flour. Sprinkle one fourth of the sugar mixture evenly over the bottom of the crust. Add the peaches, cherries, almond extract, and lemon juice to the remaining sugar mixture. Turn the filling into the crust and dot with butter. Roll out, cut, and lay on the lattice strips. After the pie is latticed and crimped, sprinkle 1 tablespoon of sugar over the lattice crust.

Bake 40 to 45 minutes or until golden brown.

NO. 98   **PEACH BLACKBERRY PIE**
                          One 9-inch lattice-top pie

Follow the recipe for Peach Cherry Pie (No. 97), substituting fresh
blackberries for cherries. Bake as directed.

NO. 99   **PEAR GINGER PIE**
                          One 9-inch double-crust pie

Pastry for a 9-inch double-crust pie
(Classic Double Crust)

½ cup dark brown sugar,
    firmly packed
	5 cups peeled, cored, and
	    sliced Bosc pears

3 tablespoons flour	¼ cup candied ginger, coarsely chopped
1 tablespoon grated lemon zest	3 tablespoons lemon juice
¼ teaspoon ground ginger	4 tablespoons unsalted
¼ teaspoon nutmeg	butter or margarine

Preheat the oven to 450° F. Prepare the pie pastry. Line the pie
pan with the bottom crust, using half of the dough. Keep the
remaining dough chilled.

Combine the sugar, flour, lemon zest, ginger, and nutmeg. Mix
well. Add the pears, candied ginger, and lemon juice. Mix well.
Turn the filling into the crust and dot with butter. Roll out the
top crust and lay it on the filling. Trim off any excess dough, crimp
the edges, and prick with the tines of a fork to vent.

Bake at 450° F for 10 minutes. Reduce the heat to 350° F and
bake about 30 minutes more or until golden brown.

NO. 100   **PLUM GINGER PIE**
                          One 9-inch double-crust pie

Follow the recipe for Pear Ginger Pie (No. 99), substituting plums
for pears. Bake as directed.

NO. 101   # MOCK CHERRY PIE

One 9-inch double-crust pie

Pastry for a 9-inch double-crust pie
(Classic Double Crust)

1 cup sugar
2 tablespoons flour
3 cups cranberries, coarsely
   chopped
1 cup raisins

¼ cup orange juice
½ cup water
½ teaspoon vanilla extract
2 tablespoons unsalted
   butter or margarine

Preheat the oven to 450° F. Prepare the pie pastry. Line the pie pan with the bottom crust, using half of the dough. Keep the remaining dough chilled.

Mix together the sugar and flour. Add the cranberries, raisins, orange juice, water, and vanilla. Turn the filling into the crust and dot with butter. Roll out the top crust and lay it on the filling. Trim off any excess dough, crimp the edges, and prick with the tines of a fork to vent.

Bake at 450° F for 10 minutes. Reduce the heat to 350° F and bake 35 to 40 minutes more or until golden brown.

NO. 102   # RAISIN BLACKBERRY PIE

One 9-inch double-crust pie

Pastry for a 9-inch double-crust pie
(Classic Double Crust)

⅔ cup sugar
1 tablespoon cornstarch
½ teaspoon allspice
1½ cups raisins
1¾ cups blackberries

1 cup blackberry or cherry
   juice
1 tablespoon lemon juice
2 tablespoons unsalted
   butter or margarine

Preheat the oven to 450° F. Prepare the pie pastry. Line the pie pan with the bottom crust, using half of the dough. Keep the remaining dough chilled.

Mix together the sugar, cornstarch, and allspice. Add the raisins, blackberries, blackberry juice, and lemon juice. Turn the filling into the crust and dot with butter. Roll out the top crust and lay it on the filling. Trim off any excess dough, crimp the edges, and prick with the tines of a fork to vent.

Bake at 450° F for 10 minutes. Reduce the heat to 350° F and bake 25 to 30 minutes more or until golden brown.

NO. 103   **RED CURRANT RASPBERRY PIE**

One 9-inch lattice-top pie

Pastry for a 9-inch lattice-top pie
(Classic Double Crust)

1 cup dark brown sugar, firmly packed
3 tablespoons flour
1 teaspoon cinnamon
½ teaspoon allspice
3 cups fresh raspberries

1 cup red currants
1 tablespoon lemon juice
1 teaspoon grated lemon zest
2 teaspoons unsalted butter or margarine
1 tablespoon sugar

Preheat the oven to 450° F. Prepare the pie pastry. Line the pie pan with the bottom crust, using half of the dough. Keep the remaining dough chilled.

Mix together the brown sugar, flour, cinnamon, and allspice. Sprinkle one fourth of the sugar mixture evenly over the bottom of the crust. Add to the remaining sugar mixture the raspberries, currants, lemon juice, and lemon zest. Mix well. Turn the filling into the crust and dot with butter. Roll out, cut, and lay on the lattice strips. After the pie is latticed and crimped, sprinkle 1 tablespoon of sugar over the lattice crust.

Bake at 450° F for 10 minutes. Reduce the heat to 350° F and bake 35 to 40 minutes more or until golden brown.

NO. 104   **RHUBARB STRAWBERRY PIE**

One 9-inch lattice-top pie

Pastry for a 9-inch lattice-top pie
(Classic Double Crust)

¼ cup flour
2 tablespoons cornstarch
1 cup light brown sugar,
    firmly packed
½ teaspoon allspice
1½ cups diced fresh rhubarb
1½ cups halved fresh
    strawberries

2 tablespoons lemon juice
1 teaspoon grated lemon
    zest
2 tablespoons unsalted
    butter or margarine
1 tablespoon sugar

Preheat the oven to 450° F. Prepare the pie pastry. Line the pie pan with the bottom crust, using half of the dough. Keep the remaining dough chilled.

Mix together the flour, cornstarch, brown sugar, and allspice. Sprinkle one fourth of the flour mixture evenly over the bottom of the crust. Combine the remaining flour mixture with the rhubarb, strawberries, lemon juice, and lemon zest. Mix well. Turn the filling into the crust and dot with butter. Roll out, cut, and lay on the lattice strips. After the pie is latticed and crimped, sprinkle 1 tablespoon of sugar over the lattice crust.

Bake at 450° F for 10 minutes. Reduce the heat to 350° F and bake 30 minutes more or until golden brown.

NO. 105   **STRAWBERRY PEACH PIE**

One 9-inch double-crust pie

Pastry for a 9-inch double-crust pie
(Classic Double Crust)

⅓ cup sugar
¼ cup uncooked tapioca
¼ teaspoon cinnamon
¼ teaspoon nutmeg

⅛ teaspoon salt
4 cups peeled, sliced
    peaches
1 cup fresh sliced
    strawberries

Preheat the oven to 400° F. Prepare the pie pastry. Line the pie pan with the bottom crust, using half of the dough. Keep the remaining dough chilled.

Combine the sugar, tapioca, cinnamon, nutmeg, and salt. Add the peaches and strawberries and mix well. Turn the filling into the crust. Roll out the top crust and lay it on the filling. Trim off any excess dough, crimp the edges, and prick with the tines of a fork to vent.

Bake 50 minutes or until golden brown.

NO. 106 **STRAWBERRY PEACH MERINGUE PIE**

One 9-inch single-crust pie

Recipe for Strawberry Peach Pie (No. 105)

Meringue

3 large egg whites, at room temperature
½ teaspoon vanilla extract

¼ teaspoon cream of tartar
6 tablespoons superfine sugar

Prepare the recipe for Strawberry Peach Pie, substituting the Classic Single Crust for the Classic Double Crust. Trim and crimp the edges, then fill and bake as directed.

While the pie is still hot, prepare the meringue. Preheat the oven to 350° F. Beat the egg whites, vanilla, and cream of tartar until the mixture holds stiff peaks. Gradually add the sugar, 1 tablespoon at a time, beating until very stiff and glossy. All the sugar must be dissolved. Spread the meringue over the hot pie filling, sealing it to the edge of the crust. Bake 12 to 15 minutes or until golden brown. Cool before serving.

NO. 107 **RASPBERRY PEACH PIE**

One 9-inch double-crust pie

Follow the recipe for Strawberry Peach Pie (No. 105), substituting raspberries for strawberries. Bake as directed.

NO. 108   **RASPBERRY PEACH MERINGUE PIE**

One 9-inch single-crust pie

Recipe for Strawberry Peach Pie (No. 105)

Meringue

3 large egg whites, at room
    temperature
½ teaspoon vanilla extract

¼ teaspoon cream of tartar
6 tablespoons superfine
    sugar

Prepare the recipe for Strawberry Peach Pie, substituting the Classic Single Crust for the Classic Double Crust, and using raspberries in place of strawberries. Trim and crimp the edges, then fill and bake as directed.

While the pie is still hot, prepare the meringue. Preheat the oven to 350° F. Beat the egg whites, vanilla, and cream of tartar until the mixture holds stiff peaks. Gradually add the sugar, 1 tablespoon at a time, beating until very stiff and glossy. All the sugar must be dissolved. Spread the meringue over the pie filling, sealing it to the edge of the crust. Bake 12 to 15 minutes or until golden brown. Cool before serving.

NO. 109   **SPRING PIE**

One 9-inch lattice-top pie

Pastry for a 9-inch lattice-top pie
(Classic Double Crust)

1½ cups plus 1 tablespoon
    sugar
⅓ cup flour
1 tablespoon uncooked
    tapioca
1½ cups sliced fresh
    strawberries

1½ cups diced fresh rhubarb
1½ cups diced pineapple
2 tablespoons unsalted
    butter or margarine

Preheat the oven to 450° F. Prepare the pie pastry. Line the pie pan with the bottom crust, using half of the dough. Keep the remaining dough chilled.

Combine 1½ cups of the sugar, flour, and tapioca. Sprinkle one fourth of the sugar mixture evenly over the bottom of the crust. Add the remaining sugar mixture to the strawberries, rhubarb, and pineapple. Mix well. Turn the filling into the crust and dot with butter. Roll out, cut, and lay on the lattice strips. After the pie is latticed and crimped, sprinkle 1 tablespoon of sugar over the lattice crust.

Bake at 450° F for 10 minutes. Reduce the heat to 350° F and bake 35 to 40 minutes more or until golden brown.

NO. 110   **SUMMER PIE**

One 9-inch lattice-top pie

Pastry for a 9-inch lattice-top pie
(Classic Double Crust)

    1 cup plus 1 tablespoon   ½ cup red currants
       sugar   1 cup pitted halved sour red
    3 tablespoons flour   cherries
    1½ cups raspberries   2 tablespoons unsalted
                                   butter or margarine

Preheat the oven to 450° F. Prepare the pie pastry. Line the pie pan with the bottom crust, using half of the dough. Keep the remaining dough chilled.

Combine 1 cup of the sugar with the flour. Sprinkle one fourth of the sugar mixture evenly over the bottom of the crust. Add the raspberries, currants, and cherries to the remaining sugar mixture. Turn the filling into the crust and dot with butter. Roll out, cut, and lay on the lattice strips. After the pie is latticed and crimped, sprinkle 1 tablespoon of sugar over the lattice crust.

Bake at 450° F for 10 minutes. Reduce the heat to 350° F and bake 30 minutes more or until golden brown.

NO. 111   **AUTUMN PIE**

One 9-inch single-crust pie

Prebaked 9-inch pie shell
(Classic Single Crust or Graham Cracker Crust)

4 plums, peeled and sliced   ½ cup light brown sugar,
2 pears, peeled, cored, and   firmly packed
   sliced   1 teaspoon lemon juice
1 cup seedless green grapes   ¼ teaspoon almond extract
8 peaches, peeled and sliced   Sweetened whipped cream

Prepare the prebaked pie shell; cool completely.

Mix together the plums, pears, grapes, peaches, sugar, lemon juice, and almond extract. Stir well. Let the mixture stand for 1 hour. Drain off the juice and turn the fruit into the pie shell. Chill until ready to serve. Serve with sweetened whipped cream.

NO. 112   **WINTER PIE**

One 9-inch single-crust pie

Prebaked 9-inch pie shell
(Classic Single Crust or Graham Cracker Crust)

1 cup dried apricots, halved   ¼ cup orange juice
1 cup dried pitted prunes,   ¼ cup lemon juice
   quartered   ¼ cup prune juice
¾ cup sugar   ¼ cup apricot juice
¼ cup flour   Sweetened whipped cream
⅛ teaspoon salt

Combine the apricots and prunes. Cover with cold water and let stand overnight.

The next day, prepare the prebaked pie shell; cool completely.

In a large saucepan, combine the sugar, flour, and salt. Stir in the fruit juices and bring to a boil. Reduce the heat to low and cook, stirring frequently, for 10 minutes. Remove the pan from the heat. Arrange the fruit in the pie shell. Pour the glaze over the fruit. Chill until ready to serve. Serve with sweetened whipped cream.

Citrus Pies

There's nothing quite like a homemade lemon meringue pie—the tart filling topped with gleaming, sugary meringue resting in a crisply browned crust. Or how about a cool Key Lime pie on a hot summer night? Lemons, limes, oranges, and grapefruit are the main ingredients of this delectable collection of citrus pies. Anyone looking for a citrus shortcut should turn to the Quick-and-Easy Pies chapter, where commercial mixes are substituted for homemade fillings.

GRAPEFRUIT PIE

One 9-inch single-crust pie

Prebaked 9-inch pie shell
(Classic Single Crust or Graham Cracker Crust)

1 cup grapefruit juice	3 tablespoons cornstarch
¼ cup orange juice	2 egg yolks, beaten
1 tablespoon lemon juice	1 tablespoon butter
1 cup sugar	1 teaspoon grated grapefruit
½ cup water	zest

Meringue

3 large egg whites, at room temperature	¼ teaspoon cream of tartar
½ teaspoon vanilla extract	6 tablespoons superfine sugar

Prepare the prebaked pie shell; cool completely.

In the top of a double boiler over simmering water, heat the fruit juices and sugar. Mix together the water and cornstarch and add to the fruit juice. Cook, stirring frequently, for 20 minutes or until thickened. Stir a small amount of the fruit mixture into the egg yolks. Combine the egg yolk mixture with the mixture in the double boiler. Add the butter. Cook for 2 minutes more. Remove the pan from the heat. Stir in the grapefruit zest. Turn the filling into the pie shell.

Preheat the oven to 350° F. Prepare the meringue. Beat the egg whites, vanilla, and cream of tartar until the mixture holds stiff peaks. Gradually add the sugar, 1 tablespoon at a time, beating until very stiff and glossy. All the sugar must be dissolved. Spread the meringue over the hot filling, sealing it to the edge of the crust. Bake for 12 to 15 minutes or until golden brown. Cool before serving.

NO. 114   **KEY LIME PIE I**

One 9-inch single-crust pie

Prebaked 9-inch pie shell
(Classic Single Crust or Graham Cracker Crust)

3 egg yolks   Juice of 3 limes, preferably
1¾ cups sweetened condensed   Key limes
    milk   1 tablespoon sugar

Meringue

3 large egg whites, at room   ¼ teaspoon cream of tartar
    temperature   6 tablespoons superfine
½ teaspoon vanilla extract   sugar

Prepare the prebaked pie shell; cool completely.

Beat the egg yolks until thick and light. Beat in the condensed milk, lime juice, and sugar. Turn the filling into the pie shell.

Preheat the oven to 350° F. To prepare the meringue, beat the egg whites, vanilla, and cream of tartar until the mixture holds stiff peaks. Gradually add the sugar, 1 tablespoon at a time, beating until very stiff and glossy. All the sugar must be dissolved. Spread the meringue over the filling, sealing it to the edge of the crust. Bake 12 to 15 minutes or until golden brown. Cool before serving.

NO. 115   **KEY LIME PIE II**

One 9-inch single-crust pie

Prebaked 9-inch pie shell
(Classic Single Crust or Graham Cracker Crust)

5 egg yolks   2 teaspoons grated lime zest
1 cup sweetened condensed   1 tablespoon sugar
    milk
½ cup lime juice, preferably
    from Key limes

Meringue

3 large egg whites, at room   ¼ teaspoon cream of tartar
    temperature   6 tablespoons superfine
½ teaspoon vanilla extract   sugar

Prepare the prebaked pie shell; cool completely. Preheat the oven to 350° F.

Beat the egg yolks until thick and light. Beat in the condensed milk, lime juice, lime zest, and sugar. Turn the filling into the pie shell.

Bake 15 minutes. Remove the pie from the oven and leave the oven on.

While the pie is still hot, prepare the meringue. Beat the egg whites, vanilla, and cream of tartar until the mixture holds stiff peaks. Gradually add the sugar, 1 tablespoon at a time, beating until very stiff and glossy. All the sugar must be dissolved. Spread the meringue over the pie filling, sealing it to the edge of the crust. Bake for 12 to 15 minutes or until golden brown. Cool before serving.

NO. 116   **LEMON PIE**

One 9-inch single-crust pie

Pastry for a 9-inch single-crust pie (Classic Single Crust)

4 tablespoons unsalted butter or margarine	½ teaspoon baking soda
½ cup light brown sugar, firmly packed	⅛ teaspoon nutmeg
1 large egg	2 tablespoons lemon juice
¼ cup flour	1 teaspoon grated lemon zest

Preheat the oven to 425° F. Prepare the pie pastry. Line the pie pan with the dough. Trim and crimp the edges.

Cream together the butter and sugar. Add the egg and beat well. Combine the flour, baking soda, and nutmeg. Beat the flour mixture into the butter mixture. Stir in the lemon juice and lemon zest. Turn the filling into the crust.

Bake at 425° F for 15 minutes. Reduce the heat to 350° F and bake 25 to 30 minutes more or until the center of the pie is set.

NO. 117   **LEMON MOLASSES PIE**
                                  One 9-inch lattice-top pie

**Pastry for a 9-inch lattice-top pie
(Classic Double Crust)**

1½ cups plus 1 tablespoon   2 cups water
   sugar   ¼ cup dark molasses
¼ cup flour   ⅓ cup lemon juice
5 tablespoons cornstarch   2 teaspoons grated lemon
¼ teaspoon nutmeg   zest
½ teaspoon salt

Preheat the oven to 450° F. Prepare the pie pastry. Line the pie pan with the bottom crust, using half of the dough. Keep the remaining dough chilled.

Mix together 1½ cups of the sugar, flour, cornstarch, nutmeg, and salt. Bring the water to a boil. Add the molasses, lemon juice, and lemon zest. In the top of a double boiler set over simmering water, combine the sugar mixture and the molasses mixture. Cook, stirring constantly, for 20 minutes or until thickened. Remove the pan from the heat. Turn the filling into the crust. Roll out, cut, and lay on the lattice strips. After the pie is latticed and crimped, sprinkle 1 tablespoon of sugar over the lattice crust.

Bake at 450° F for 10 minutes. Reduce the heat to 350° F and bake 30 minutes more or until golden brown.

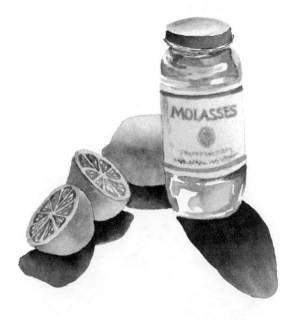

NO. 118 ## ORANGE MOLASSES PIE
One 9-inch lattice-top pie

Follow the recipe for Lemon Molasses Pie (No. 117), substituting orange juice and orange zest for lemon juice and lemon zest. Reduce the quantity of sugar to 1 cup. Bake as directed.

NO. 119 ## LEMON MERINGUE PIE I
One 9-inch single-crust pie

Prebaked 9-inch pie shell
(Classic Single Crust)
1½ cups water
¾ cup sugar
2 teaspoons grated lemon
    zest
3 tablespoons cornstarch

2 egg yolks, beaten
2 tablespoons unsalted
    butter or margarine
6 tablespoons lemon juice

Meringue

3 large egg whites, at room
    temperature
½ teaspoon vanilla extract

¼ teaspoon cream of tartar
6 tablespoons superfine
    sugar

Prepare the prebaked pie shell; cool completely.

In the top of a double boiler set over simmering water, combine 1 cup of the water, the sugar, and lemon zest. Bring the mixture to a boil. Mix the cornstarch with the remaining water and add to the hot mixture. Cook, stirring frequently for 20 minutes or until thickened. Stir a small amount of the lemon mixture into the egg yolks. Combine the egg yolk mixture with the mixture in the double boiler. Cook for 2 minutes more. Remove the pan from the heat. Stir in the butter. Add the lemon juice. Turn the filling into the pie shell.

While the filling is still hot, prepare the meringue. Preheat the oven to 350° F. Beat the egg whites, vanilla, and cream of tartar until the mixture holds stiff peaks. Gradually add the sugar, 1 tablespoon at a time, beating until very stiff and glossy. All the sugar must be dissolved. Spread the meringue over the hot filling, sealing it to the edge of the crust. Bake 12 to 15 minutes or until golden brown. Cool before serving.

NO. 120   **LEMON MERINGUE PIE II**
                        One 9-inch single-crust pie

Prebaked 9-inch pie shell
(Classic Single Crust)
  2 cups milk
  ⅓ cup cornstarch
  1 cup sugar
  3 egg yolks, beaten

  ⅓ cup lemon juice
  1 teaspoon grated lemon
    zest
  2 tablespoons unsalted
    butter or margarine

Meringue
  3 large egg whites, at room
    temperature
  ½ teaspoon vanilla extract

  ¼ teaspoon cream of tartar
  6 tablespoons superfine
    sugar

Prepare the prebaked pie shell; cool completely.

In the top of a double boiler set over simmering water, scald the milk. Mix together the cornstarch and sugar. Pour the hot milk over the cornstarch mixture, stirring constantly. Return the mixture to the double boiler. Cook, stirring frequently, for 20 minutes or until thickened. Stir a small amount of the hot custard into the egg yolks. Combine the egg yolk mixture with the mixture in the double boiler. Cook for 2 minutes more. Remove the pan from the heat. Stir in the lemon juice, lemon zest, and butter. Turn the filling into the pie shell.

Preheat the oven to 350° F. While the filling is still hot, prepare the meringue. Beat the egg whites, vanilla, and cream of tartar until the mixture holds stiff peaks. Gradually add the sugar, 1 tablespoon at a time, beating until very stiff and glossy. All the sugar must be dissolved. Spread the meringue over the hot filling, sealing it to the edge of the crust. Bake 12 to 15 minutes or until golden brown. Cool before serving.

NO. 121   # LEMON SLICE PIE

One 9-inch lattice-top pie

Pastry for a 9-inch lattice-top pie
(Classic Double Crust)

1½ cups plus 1 tablespoon sugar	½ cup thinly sliced, peeled and seeded lemons
¾ cup flour	1 cup cold water
2 teaspoons grated lemon zest	1 tablespoon unsalted butter or margarine

Preheat the oven to 450° F. Prepare the pie pastry. Line the pie pan with the bottom crust, using half of the dough. Keep the remaining dough chilled.

Combine the sugar, flour, and lemon zest. Sprinkle 1½ cups of the sugar mixture evenly over the bottom of the crust. Arrange the lemon slices on top of the sugar mixture. Combine the water with the remaining sugar mixture and pour over the lemon slices. Dot with butter. Roll out, cut, and lay on the lattice strips. After the pie is latticed and crimped, sprinkle 1 tablespoon of sugar over the lattice crust.

Bake at 450° F for 10 minutes. Reduce the heat to 350° F and bake 35 to 40 minutes more or until golden brown.

NO. 122   # ORANGE SLICE PIE

One 9-inch lattice-top pie

Follow the recipe for Lemon Slice Pie (No. 121), substituting oranges, orange juice, and orange zest for lemons, lemon juice and lemon zest. Reduce the quantity of sugar to ¾ cup. Bake as directed.

NO. 123   ## LEMON SOUFFLÉ PIE
                                 One 9-inch single-crust pie

Prebaked 9-inch pie shell
(Classic Single Crust)
  1 teaspoon grated lemon   3 eggs, separated
     zest   ⅓ cup lemon juice
  3 tablespoons water
  1 cup sugar

Prepare the prebaked pie shell; cool completely. Preheat the oven to 300° F.

In the top of a double boiler set over simmering water, combine the lemon zest, water, ½ cup of the sugar, and egg yolks. Cook, stirring frequently, for about 20 minutes or until thickened. Remove the pan from the heat. Stir in the lemon juice. In a separate bowl, beat the egg whites until they form stiff peaks. Beat in the remaining sugar. Gently fold the egg white mixture into the custard. Turn the filling into the pie shell.

Bake about 40 minutes or until the center of the pie is set.

NO. 124   ## ORANGE SOUFFLÉ PIE
                                 One 9-inch single-crust pie

Follow the recipe for Lemon Soufflé Pie (No. 123), substituting orange juice and orange zest for lemon juice and lemon zest, and using only ¼ cup of sugar in the custard mixture. Bake as directed.

NO. 125   ## LEMON SPONGE PIE
                                 One 9-inch single-crust pie

Pastry for a 9-inch single-crust pie
(Classic Single Crust)
  2 eggs, separated   1 cup milk
  1 cup sugar   2 tablespoons flour
    Juice and grated zest of 1   1 tablespoon melted butter
      large lemon

Preheat the oven to 450° F. Prepare the pie pastry. Line the pie pan with the dough. Trim and crimp the edges.

Beat the egg yolks until light and thick. Beat in the sugar. Beat in the lemon juice, lemon zest, milk, and flour. Add the melted butter. In a separate bowl, beat the egg whites until they form stiff peaks. Gently fold the egg whites into the egg yolk mixture. Turn the filling into the crust.

Bake at 450° F for 10 minutes. Reduce the heat to 325° F and bake 20 minutes more.

NO. 126 ## ORANGE SPONGE PIE

One 9-inch single-crust pie

Follow the recipe for Lemon Sponge Pie (No. 125), substituting 1 tablespoon of grated orange zest and ¼ cup of orange juice for the lemon juice and zest. Reduce the quantity of sugar to ½ cup. Bake as directed.

NO. 127 ## ORANGE MERINGUE PIE I

One 9-inch single-crust pie

Prebaked 9-inch pie shell
(Classic Single Crust or Graham Cracker Crust)

¼ cup flour	1 cup orange juice
¾ cup sugar	1 tablespoon lemon juice
½ cup water	2 tablespoons unsalted
2 teaspoons grated orange	butter or margarine
zest	2 egg yolks, beaten

Meringue

3 large egg whites, at room	¼ teaspoon cream of tartar
temperature	6 tablespoons superfine
½ teaspoon vanilla extract	sugar

Prepare the prebaked pie shell; cool completely. Preheat the oven to 350° F.

In the top of a double boiler set over simmering water, combine the flour, sugar, and water. Add the orange zest, orange juice, and lemon juice. Cook, stirring frequently, for 20 minutes or until thickened. Remove the pan from the heat. Add the butter. Stir a small amount of the orange mixture into the egg yolks. Combine the egg yolk mixture with the mixture in the top of the double boiler. Cook 2 minutes more. Remove the pan from the heat. Turn the filling into the pie shell.

While the filling is still hot, prepare the meringue. Preheat the oven to 350° F. Beat the egg whites, vanilla, and cream of tartar until the mixture holds stiff peaks. Gradually add the sugar, 1 tablespoon at a time, beating until very stiff and glossy. All the sugar must be dissolved. Spread the meringue over the hot filling, sealing it to the edge of the crust. Bake 12 to 15 minutes or until golden brown.

NO. 128   # ORANGE MERINGUE PIE II

One 9-inch single-crust pie

**Prebaked 9-inch pie shell
(Classic Single Crust)**

1¼ cups sugar	¾ cup orange juice
3 tablespoons flour	2 teaspoons grated orange zest
2 tablespoons cornstarch	
1 cup milk, scalded	2 tablespoons lemon juice
3 egg yolks, beaten	2 tablespoons unsalted butter or margarine

Meringue

3 large egg whites, at room temperature	¼ teaspoon cream of tartar
½ teaspoon vanilla extract	6 tablespoons superfine sugar

Prepare the prebaked pie shell; cool completely.

In the top of a double boiler set over simmering water, combine the sugar, flour, cornstarch, and milk. Cook, stirring frequently, for 20 minutes or until thickened. Stir a small amount of the hot custard into the egg yolks. Combine the egg yolk mixture with the mixture in the double boiler. Cook for 2 minutes more. Remove the pan from the heat. Stir in the orange juice, orange zest, lemon juice, and butter. Turn the filling into the pie shell.

Preheat the oven to 350° F. While the filling is still hot, prepare the meringue. Beat the egg whites, vanilla, and cream of tartar until the mixture holds stiff peaks. Gradually add the sugar, 1 tablespoon at a time, beating until very stiff and glossy. All the sugar must be dissolved. Spread the meringue over the hot filling, sealing it to the edge of the crust. Bake 12 to 15 minutes or until golden brown.

NO. 129   **ORANGE PECAN CREAM PIE**

One 9-inch single-crust pie

Follow the recipe for Orange Meringue Pie II (No. 128), omitting the meringue and adding ½ cup of coarsely chopped pecans to the hot custard. Refrigerate until ready to serve. Serve with sweetened whipped cream.

NO. 130   **ORANGE MARSHMALLOW MERINGUE PIE**

One 9-inch single-crust pie

Follow the recipe for Orange Meringue Pie II (No. 128), adding 10 quartered marshmallows to the hot custard. Bake as directed.

NO. 131   **SHAKER LEMON SLICE PIE**

One 9-inch double-crust pie

**Pastry for a 9-inch double-crust pie
(Classic Double Crust)**

3 medium-size thin-skinned lemons	4 eggs, beaten
2 cups sugar	¼ teaspoon nutmeg

Slice the whole lemons paper thin. Combine the lemons and sugar and let the mixture stand overnight.

The next day, preheat the oven to 450° F. Prepare the pie pastry. Line the pie pan with the bottom crust, using half of the dough. Keep the remaining dough chilled.

Add the eggs and nutmeg to the lemon mixture. Mix well. Turn the filling into the crust. Roll out the top crust and lay it on the filling. Trim off any excess dough, crimp the edges, and prick with the tines of a fork to vent.

Bake at 450° F for 15 minutes. Reduce the heat to 375° F and bake about 20 minutes more or until golden brown.

NO. 132   **LIME SLICE PIE**
One 9-inch double-crust pie

Follow the recipe for Shaker Lemon Slice Pie (No. 131), substituting 4 thin-skinned limes for the 3 lemons. Bake as directed.

Cream and Custard Pies

From apricot cream to maple praline and from chocolate chess to a sour cream butterscotch extravaganza, these cream and custard pies are for serious sugar-lovers. Cream pies, with their prebaked pie shells and luscious cooked fillings, are the perfect outlet for creative cooking with special crusts made with cocoa, walnuts, or spices. (The crust chapter offers a selection of special recipes that will be delicious with your favorite cream or custard pie.) Baked custard pies are often called "cream" pies, but the true distinction between cream and custard pies is that the cream (or milk) is cooked and the custard is baked. To prevent spoilage, always keep cream and custard pies refrigerated until serving.

APRICOT CREAM PIE

One 9-inch single-crust pie

Prebaked 9-inch pie shell
(Classic Single Crust or Graham Cracker Crust)

2 cups dried apricots	2 egg yolks, beaten
2 cups cold water	2 tablespoons unsalted
½ cup sugar	butter or margarine
¼ cup flour	Sweetened whipped cream
¾ cup milk, scalded	Chocolate shavings

Prepare the prebaked pie shell; cool completely.

Combine the apricots and water in a saucepan and soak for 30 minutes. Bring the mixture to a boil. Reduce the heat to low and simmer for 10 minutes. Remove the pan from the heat and drain. Reduce the apricots to a fine pulp in a food processor.

In the top of a double boiler set over simmering water, mix together the sugar and flour. Slowly stir in the hot milk and apricot pulp. Cook, stirring frequently, for 20 minutes or until thickened. Stir a small amount of the apricot mixture into the egg yolks. Combine the egg yolk mixture with the mixture in the double boiler. Cook for 2 minutes more. Remove the pan from the heat. Stir in the butter. Turn the filling into the pie shell.

Chill until serving. Decorate with sweetened whipped cream and chocolate shavings.

APRICOT BANANA CREAM PIE

One 9-inch single-crust pie

Recipe for Apricot Cream Pie (No. 133)
1 cup sliced firm, ripe
bananas

Meringue

3 large egg whites, at room temperature	¼ teaspoon cream of tartar
½ teaspoon vanilla extract	6 tablespoons superfine sugar

Prepare the recipe for Apricot Cream Pie, adding 1 cup of sliced bananas to the hot custard.

While the filling is still hot, prepare the meringue. Preheat the oven to 350° F. Beat the egg whites, vanilla, and cream of tartar until the mixture holds stiff peaks. Gradually add the sugar, 1 tablespoon at a time, beating until very stiff and glossy. All the sugar must be dissolved. Spread the meringue over the hot filling, sealing it to the edge of the crust. Bake 12 to 15 minutes or until golden brown. Chill until serving.

NO. 135   **FLUFFY APRICOT PIE**

One 9-inch single-crust pie

Prebaked 9-inch pie shell
(Classic Single Crust or Graham Cracker Crust)

2 cups dried apricots	1 tablespoon grated orange
2 cups cold water	zest
3 tablespoons uncooked	¼ cup orange juice
tapioca	¼ teaspoon almond extract
¼ cup sugar	¼ cup toasted slivered
2 eggs, separated	almonds

Prepare the prebaked pie shell; cool completely.

Combine the apricots and water in a saucepan and soak for 30 minutes. Bring the mixture to a boil; then reduce the heat to low and simmer for 10 minutes. Remove the pan from the heat and drain the apricots. Reduce the apricots to a fine pulp in a food processor.

Preheat the oven to 300° F. Combine the apricot pulp with the tapioca and sugar. Beat the egg yolks and stir into the mixture. Add the orange zest. Turn the mixture into the top of a double boiler set over simmering water. Cook, stirring frequently, for about 20 minutes or until thickened. Remove the pan from the heat. Stir in the orange juice and almond extract. Beat the egg whites until they form stiff peaks. Fold the egg whites into the custard. Turn the filling into the pie shell and sprinkle with toasted almonds.

Bake 15 to 20 minutes or until the custard is set. Cool, and chill until serving.

NO. 136

BANANA CREAM PIE

One 9-inch single-crust pie

Prebaked 9-inch pie shell
(Graham Cracker Crust)

  2 tablespoons unsalted
     butter or margarine
  3 tablespoons cornstarch
1½ cups milk, scalded

1 cup sugar
4 egg yolks, beaten
4 large bananas, sliced

Prepare the prebaked pie shell; cool completely.

Preheat the oven to 425° F. Melt the butter in the top of a double boiler set over simmering water. Stir in the cornstarch. Slowly stir in the hot milk, then add the sugar. Cook, stirring frequently, for 20 minutes or until thickened. Stir a small amount of the hot mixture into the egg yolks. Add the egg yolk mixture to the mixture in the double boiler. Cook for 2 minutes more. Remove the pan from the heat. Arrange the bananas in the bottom of the pie shell. Pour the hot custard over the bananas.

Bake 10 to 15 minutes or until the custard is set. Cool, and chill until serving.

NO. 137

BANANA MARSHMALLOW CREAM PIE

One 9-inch single-crust pie

Follow the recipe for Banana Cream Pie (No. 136), adding 12 quartered marshmallows to the hot custard. Bake as directed.

NO. 138   **BANANA LEMON CREAM PIE**

One 9-inch single-crust pie

Prebaked 9-inch pie shell
(Classic Single Crust or Graham Cracker Crust)

3 ounces cream cheese, at room temperature	⅓ cup lemon juice
1 egg yolk, beaten	1 teaspoon vanilla extract
1¾ cups sweetened condensed milk	3 large bananas, sliced
	¼ cup toasted slivered almonds

Prepare the prebaked pie shell; cool completely.

Beat the cream cheese until light and fluffy. Beat in the egg yolk, condensed milk, lemon juice, and vanilla. Arrange the bananas in the bottom of the pie shell. Pour the filling over the bananas. Decorate with toasted almonds. Cool, and chill until serving.

NO. 139   **BLACK WALNUT CREAM PIE**

One 9-inch single-crust pie

Prebaked 9-inch pie shell
(Classic Single Crust)

1½ cups milk, scalded	1 teaspoon grated orange zest
1 cup dark brown sugar, firmly packed	½ cup black walnuts, coarsely chopped
3 tablespoons flour	Sweetened whipped cream
2 eggs, separated	
1 tablespoon unsalted butter or margarine	

Prepare the prebaked pie shell; cool completely.

In the top of a double boiler set over simmering water, combine the milk, sugar, and flour. Cook over low heat, stirring frequently, for 20 minutes or until thickened. Beat the egg yolks. Stir a small amount of the hot custard into the egg yolks. Combine the egg yolk mixture with the mixture in the double boiler. Cook for 2 minutes more. Remove the pan from the heat. Add the butter and orange zest. Cool. Beat the egg whites until they form stiff peaks. Mix in the walnuts. Fold the mixture into the custard and turn the filling into the pie shell. Cool, and chill until serving. Serve with sweetened whipped cream.

NO. 140   **BRANDY ALEXANDER PIE**

One 9-inch single-crust pie

Prebaked 9-inch pie shell
(Graham Cracker Crust)

1½ cups milk
½ cup sugar
3 egg yolks, beaten
½ cup heavy cream
6 tablespoons cornstarch
½ cup brandy
½ cup crème de cacao
    liqueur

1 teaspoon vanilla extract
1 tablespoon unsalted butter
    or margarine
1 cup sweetened whipped
    cream
Chocolate shavings

Prepare the prebaked pie shell; cool completely.

Simmer the milk and sugar in a saucepan. In the top of a double boiler set over simmering water, combine the egg yolks, cream, and cornstarch. Stir in the hot milk mixture. Cook, stirring constantly, about 5 to 7 minutes or until the mixture is thickened. In a separate saucepan, heat the brandy, crème de cacao, and vanilla. Beat the brandy mixture into the custard, continuing to cook until thickened. Remove the pan from the heat. Stir in the butter. Cool the custard. Fold the sweetened whipped cream into the cooled custard. Turn the filling into the pie shell. Chill until serving. Decorate with chocolate shavings.

NO. 141   **BUTTERMILK PIE**

One 9-inch single-crust pie

Prebaked 9-inch pie shell
(Classic Single Crust or Graham Cracker Crust)

1 cup sugar
¼ cup flour
1 egg plus 3 egg yolks

2 cups buttermilk
1 tablespoon unsalted butter
    or margarine
1 tablespoon lemon juice

Meringue

3 large egg whites, at room
    temperature
½ teaspoon vanilla extract

¼ teaspoon cream of tartar
6 tablespoons superfine
    sugar

Prepare the prebaked pie shell; cool completely.

Mix together the sugar and flour. Beat the egg and the egg yolks and add to the sugar mixture. Stir in the buttermilk. Turn the mixture into the top of a double boiler set over simmering water. Cook, stirring frequently, about 20 minutes or until thickened. Remove the pan from the heat. Add the butter and lemon juice. Turn the filling into the pie shell.

Preheat the oven to 350° F. While the filling is still hot, prepare the meringue. Beat the egg whites, vanilla, and cream of tartar until the mixture holds stiff peaks. Gradually add the sugar, 1 tablespoon at a time, beating until very stiff and glossy. All the sugar must be dissolved. Spread the meringue over the hot filling, sealing it to the edge of the crust. Bake 12 to 15 minutes or until golden brown. Cool, and chill until serving.

NO. 142   **BUTTERSCOTCH PIE**

One 9-inch single-crust pie

Prebaked 9-inch pie shell
(Classic Single Crust or Graham Cracker Crust)

¾ cup dark brown sugar, firmly packed	1 egg plus 2 egg yolks, beaten
4 tablespoons unsalted butter or margarine	1 teaspoon vanilla extract
2 cups milk, scalded	1 teaspoon lemon juice
⅓ cup flour	

Meringue

3 large egg whites, at room temperature	¼ teaspoon cream of tartar
½ teaspoon vanilla extract	6 tablespoons superfine sugar

Prepare the prebaked pie shell; cool completely.

In the top of a double boiler set over simmering water, combine the sugar and butter. Cook, over low heat, for 2 to 3 minutes. Add 1¾ cups of the hot milk. Mix together the flour and the remaining milk. Add to the mixture in the double boiler. Cook, stirring frequently, for 20 minutes or until thickened. Stir a small amount of the hot custard into the eggs. Combine the egg mixture with the mixture in the double boiler. Cook for 2 minutes more. Remove the pan from the heat. Add the vanilla and lemon juice. Turn the filling into the pie shell.

Preheat the oven to 350° F. While the filling is still hot, prepare the meringue. Beat the egg whites, vanilla, and cream of tartar until the mixture holds stiff peaks. Gradually add the sugar, 1 tablespoon at a time, beating until very stiff and glossy. All the sugar must be dissolved. Spread the meringue over the hot filling, sealing it to the edge of the crust. Bake 12 to 15 minutes or until golden brown. Cool, and chill until serving.

NO. 143 BUTTERSCOTCH PECAN PIE
One 9-inch single-crust pie

Follow the recipe for Butterscotch Pie (No. 142), adding 1 cup of coarsely chopped pecans to the hot custard. Bake as directed.

NO. 144 BUTTERSCOTCH RAISIN PIE
One 9-inch single-crust pie

Follow the recipe for Butterscotch Pie (No. 142), adding 1 cup of raisins to the hot custard. Bake as directed.

NO. 145 CHESS PIE I
One 9-inch single-crust pie

Pastry for a 9-inch single-crust pie (Classic Single Crust)

½ cup unsalted butter or margarine, softened
1 cup sugar
3 egg yolks
1 cup raisins, coarsely chopped

1 cup walnuts, coarsely chopped
1 teaspoon vanilla extract
1 egg white
Sweetened whipped cream

Preheat the oven to 400° F. Prepare the pie pastry. Line the pie pan with the dough. Trim and crimp the edges.

Cream together the butter and sugar. Beat in the egg yolks, one at a time. Combine the egg mixture with the sugar mixture. Mix in the raisins, walnuts, and vanilla. Beat the egg white until it holds stiff peaks. Gently fold the egg white into the filling. Turn the filling into the pie shell.

Bake at 450° F for 10 minutes. Reduce the heat to 350° F and bake 30 minutes more or until the custard is set. Cool, and chill before serving. Serve with sweetened whipped cream.

NO. 146   **CHESS PIE II**

One 9-inch single-crust pie

Pastry for a 9-inch single-crust pie
(Classic Single Crust)

½ cup unsalted butter or   1 cup milk
   margarine, softened   1 teaspoon vanilla extract
2 cups sugar   2 tablespoons lemon juice
1 tablespoon flour   ¼ cup raisins, coarsely
1 tablespoon cornmeal   chopped
5 eggs, beaten   ¼ cup walnuts, coarsely
                                   chopped

Preheat the oven to 350° F. Prepare the pie pastry. Line the pie
pan with the dough. Trim and crimp the edges.

Cream together the butter and sugar. Beat in the flour and
cornmeal. Beat in the eggs, milk, vanilla, and lemon juice. Stir in
the raisins and walnuts. Turn the filling into the crust.

Bake 55 to 60 minutes or until the custard is set. Cool, and chill
before serving.

NO. 147   **LEMON CHESS PIE**

One 9-inch single-crust pie

Pastry for a 9-inch single-crust pie
(Classic Single Crust)

1 cup sugar   ⅓ cup lemon juice
½ cup light brown sugar,   2 teaspoons grated lemon
   firmly packed   zest
2 tablespoons flour   ¼ teaspoon nutmeg
5 eggs   ⅓ cup unsalted butter or
                                   margarine, melted

Preheat the oven to 325° F. Prepare the pie pastry. Line the pie
pan with the dough. Trim and crimp the edges.

Combine the sugars with the flour. Beat in the eggs, one at a
time. Add the lemon juice, lemon zest, nutmeg, and butter. Mix
well. Turn the filling into the crust.

Bake 55 to 60 minutes or until the custard is set. Cool, and chill
before serving.

NO. 148 # CHOCOLATE CHESS PIE

One 9-inch single-crust pie

Follow the recipe for Lemon Chess Pie (No. 147), adding 2 ounces of sweetened baking chocolate, melted, to the batter and substituting milk for lemon juice. Bake as directed.

NO. 149 # CHOCOLATE CREAM PIE I

One 9-inch single-crust pie

Prebaked 9-inch pie shell
(Classic Single Crust)

2 ounces (2 squares) unsweetened baking chocolate
¾ cup sugar
¼ cup flour
2 cups milk, scalded

2 egg yolks, beaten
1 teaspoon vanilla extract
2 tablespoons unsalted butter or margarine

Meringue

3 large egg whites, at room temperature
½ teaspoon vanilla extract

¼ teaspoon cream of tartar
6 tablespoons superfine sugar

Prepare the prebaked pie shell; cool completely.

Melt the chocolate in the top of a double boiler set over simmering water. Add the sugar and flour and mix well. Slowly add the hot milk to the chocolate mixture, stirring constantly. Cook, stirring frequently, for 20 minutes or until thickened. Stir a small amount of the hot custard into the egg yolks. Combine the egg yolk mixture with the mixture in the double boiler. Cook for 2 minutes more. Remove the pan from the heat. Add the vanilla and butter. Turn the filling into the pie shell.

Preheat the oven to 350° F. While the filling is still hot, prepare the meringue. Beat the egg whites, vanilla, and cream of tartar until the mixture holds stiff peaks. Gradually add the sugar, 1 tablespoon at a time, beating until very stiff and glossy. All the sugar must be dissolved. Spread the meringue over the hot filling, sealing it to the edge of the crust. Bake 12 to 15 minutes or until golden brown. Cool, and chill until serving.

NO. 150   **CHOCOLATE CREAM PIE II**

One 9-inch single-crust pie

Follow the recipe for Chocolate Cream Pie I (No. 149), omitting
the meringue topping. Decorate with sweetened whipped cream,
chocolate shavings, and candied orange peel.

NO. 151   **CHOCOLATE WALNUT CREAM PIE**

One 9-inch single-crust pie

Prebaked 9-inch pie shell
(Classic Single Crust)

3 ounces (3 squares) unsweetened baking chocolate	**1 cup hot water**
1 cup sweetened condensed milk	**2 eggs, separated**
	1 teaspoon vanilla extract
1 cup sugar	**½ cup walnuts, coarsely chopped**
¼ cup flour	**Sweetened whipped cream**
¼ teaspoon cinnamon	

Prepare the prebaked pie shell; cool completely.

In the top of a double boiler set over simmering water, melt
the chocolate with the milk. Add the sugar, flour, and cinnamon.
Slowly add the hot water to the chocolate mixture, stirring constantly. Cook, stirring frequently, for 20 minutes or until thickened.
Beat the egg yolks. Stir a small amount of the hot custard into the
egg yolks. Combine the egg yolk mixture with the mixture in the
double boiler. Cook for 2 minutes more. Remove the pan from
the heat. Add the vanilla and walnuts. Cool the custard. Beat the
egg whites until they hold stiff peaks. Fold the egg whites into
the cooled custard. Turn the filling into the pie shell. Chill until
serving. Serve with sweetened whipped cream.

NO. 152   **DOUBLE CHOCOLATE PECAN**
                                             CREAM PIE

One 9-inch single-crust pie

Follow the recipe for Chocolate Walnut Cream Pie (No. 151),
substituting pecans for walnuts and adding ½ cup of semi-sweet
chocolate morsels to the hot custard.

NO. 153

COCOA CREAM PIE
One 9-inch single-crust pie

Prebaked 9-inch pie shell
(Classic Single Crust)
- ¼ cup unsweetened cocoa powder
- 4 teaspoons cornstarch
- 1 cup sugar
- 2¼ cups milk, scalded

- 2 eggs, separated
- 2 teaspoons vanilla extract
- ¼ teaspoon cinnamon
- 8 marshmallows, quartered

Prepare the prebaked pie shell; cool completely.

In the top of a double boiler set over simmering water, combine the cocoa, cornstarch, and sugar. Slowly add the hot milk to the cocoa mixture. Cook, stirring frequently, for 20 minutes or until thickened. Beat the egg yolks. Stir a small amount of the hot custard into the egg yolks. Combine the egg yolk mixture with the mixture in the double boiler. Cook for 2 minutes more. Remove the pan from the heat. Add the vanilla, cinnamon, and marshmallows. Cool the custard. Beat the egg whites until they hold stiff peaks. Fold the egg whites into the cooled custard. Turn the filling into the pie shell. Chill until serving.

NO. 154

COCOA RAISIN CREAM PIE
One 9-inch single-crust pie

Follow the recipe for Cocoa Cream Pie (No. 153), omitting the marshmallows and adding 1 cup of raisins to the hot custard.

NO. 155

COCONUT CREAM PIE
One 9-inch single-crust pie

Prebaked 9-inch pie shell
(Classic Single Crust)
- 2 cups milk, scalded
- 3 tablespoons cornstarch
- 2 eggs
- ½ cup sugar
- 1 teaspoon vanilla extract

- ¼ teaspoon nutmeg
- 1 cup packaged unsweetened shredded coconut
- Sweetened whipped cream
- Chocolate shavings

Prepare the prebaked pie shell; cool completely.

In the top of a double boiler set over simmering water, mix ½ cup of the hot milk with the cornstarch. Add the remaining milk and cook, stirring frequently, for 20 minutes or until thickened. Beat the eggs with the sugar. Stir a small amount of the hot custard into the eggs. Combine the egg mixture with the mixture in the double boiler. Cook for 2 minutes more. Remove the pan from the heat. Add the vanilla, nutmeg, and coconut. Turn the filling into the pie shell. Chill until serving. Serve with sweetened whipped cream and chocolate shavings.

NO. 156   **FRESH COCONUT CREAM PIE**

One 9-inch single-crust pie

Follow the recipe for Coconut Cream Pie (No. 155), substituting grated fresh coconut for packaged shredded coconut and ½ cup of fresh coconut juice for ½ cup of the milk.

NO. 157   **COCONUT CREAM MERINGUE PIE**

One 9-inch single-crust pie

Recipe for Coconut Cream Pie (No. 155)

Meringue

3 large egg whites, at room
  temperature
½ teaspoon vanilla extract

¼ teaspoon cream of tartar
6 tablespoons superfine
  sugar

Prepare the recipe for Coconut Cream Pie.

While the filling is still hot, prepare the meringue. Preheat the oven to 350° F. Beat the egg whites, vanilla, and cream of tartar until the mixture holds stiff peaks. Gradually add the sugar, 1 tablespoon at a time, beating until very stiff and glossy. All the sugar must be dissolved. Spread the meringue over the hot filling, sealing it to the edge of the crust. Bake 12 to 15 minutes or until golden brown. Cool, and chill until serving.

NO. 158   COCONUT MOLASSES PIE

One 9-inch single-crust pie

Pastry for a 9-inch single-crust pie
(Classic Single Crust)
 ¼ cup flour   ½ cup dark molasses
 ½ cup dark brown sugar,   ¼ cup sour cream
   firmly packed   ½ cup milk
 ½ cup packaged unsweetened   1 teaspoon vanilla extract
   shredded coconut   2 eggs, beaten
 ¼ teaspoon baking soda
 ¼ teaspoon nutmeg

Preheat the oven to 350° F. Prepare the pie pastry. Line the pie
pan with the dough. Trim and crimp the edges.

Mix together the flour, sugar, coconut, baking soda, and nutmeg.
Add the molasses, sour cream, milk, vanilla, and eggs. Mix well.
Turn the filling into the crust.

Bake at 350° F for 10 minutes. Reduce the heat to 325° F and
bake 35 to 40 minutes more or until the custard is set. Cool, and
chill until serving.

NO. 159   COFFEE CREAM PIE

One 9-inch single-crust pie

Prebaked 9-inch pie shell
(Classic Single Crust)
 1½ cups hot, freshly brewed   ¾ cup sugar
    coffee   ⅓ cup flour
  2 ounces (2 squares)   3 egg yolks, beaten
    unsweetened baking   1 teaspoon vanilla extract
    chocolate   ¼ teaspoon cinnamon
 ½ cup heavy cream   Sweetened whipped cream

Prepare the prebaked pie shell; cool completely.

In the top of a double boiler set over simmering water, combine
the coffee and chocolate. When the chocolate is melted, mix together the cream, sugar, and flour. Stir the cream mixture into
the coffee mixture. Cook, stirring frequently, for 20 minutes or
until thickened. Stir a small amount of the hot custard into the
egg yolks. Combine the egg yolk mixture with the mixture in the

double boiler. Cook for 5 minutes more. Remove the pan from the heat. Add the vanilla and cinnamon. Turn the filling into the pie shell. Cool, and chill until serving. Serve with sweetened whipped cream.

NO. 160   # COTTAGE CHEESE PIE

One 9-inch single-crust pie

Pastry for a 9-inch single-crust pie
(Classic Single Crust)

1 cup cottage cheese	¾ cup sugar
4 eggs, separated	¼ cup lemon juice
1¼ cups heavy cream	1 tablespoon grated lemon
1 tablespoon flour	zest
½ cup dried currants	Confectioners' sugar

Preheat the oven to 450° F. Prepare the pie pastry. Line the pie pan with the dough. Trim and crimp the edges.

Drain the cottage cheese, pressing it through a sieve. Beat the egg yolks. Combine the cottage cheese with the egg yolks, cream, and flour. Mix in the currants, sugar, lemon juice, and lemon zest. Beat the egg whites until they hold stiff peaks. Gently fold the egg whites into the cottage cheese mixture. Turn the filling into the crust.

Bake at 450° F for 10 minutes. Reduce the heat to 350° F and bake 45 minutes more or until golden brown. While still warm, sprinkle with confectioners' sugar.

NO. 161   # CRAB APPLE CUSTARD PIE

One 9-inch single-crust pie

Pastry for a 9-inch single-crust pie
(Classic Single Crust)

2 cups peeled, cored, and sliced crab apples	1 teaspoon vanilla extract
⅔ cup sugar	1 cup milk
1 tablespoon flour	1 cup heavy cream
3 egg yolks, beaten	

Preheat the oven to 450° F. Prepare the pie pastry. Line the pie pan with the dough. Trim and crimp the edges.

Arrange the crab apples in the bottom of the crust. Combine the sugar, flour, egg yolks, vanilla, milk, and cream. Mix well, and pour over the crab apples.

Bake at 450° F for 15 minutes. Reduce the heat to 325° F and bake 30 minutes more or until the custard is set. Cool, and chill until serving.

NO. 162

DATE CREAM PIE

One 9-inch single-crust pie

**Prebaked 9-inch pie shell
(Classic Single Crust)**
1½ cups milk, scalded
4 tablespoons sugar
⅓ cup flour
2 egg yolks, beaten

2 cups pitted dates, coarsely chopped
2 tablespoons peanut butter
1 teaspoon lemon juice

Meringue

3 large egg whites, at room temperature
½ teaspoon vanilla extract

¼ teaspoon cream of tartar
6 tablespoons superfine sugar

Prepare the prebaked pie shell; cool completely.

In the top of a double boiler set over simmering water, combine 1 cup of the hot milk with the sugar and flour. Add the remaining milk and cook, stirring frequently, for 20 minutes or until thickened. Stir a small amount of the hot custard into the egg yolks. Combine the egg yolk mixture with the mixture in the double boiler. Cook for 2 minutes more. Remove the pan from the heat. Add the dates, peanut butter, and lemon juice. Turn the filling into the pie shell.

Preheat the oven to 350° F. While the filling is still hot, prepare the meringue. Beat the egg whites, vanilla, and cream of tartar until the mixture holds stiff peaks. Gradually add the sugar, 1 tablespoon at a time, beating until very stiff and glossy. All the sugar must be dissolved. Spread the meringue over the hot filling, sealing it to the edge of the crust. Bake 12 to 15 minutes or until golden brown. Cool, and chill until serving.

NO. 163   **FRANGIPANI CREAM PIE**

One 9-inch single-crust pie

Prebaked 9-inch pie shell
(Walnut Crust)
  2 cups milk, scalded
  1 cup sugar
  ⅓ cup flour
  2 eggs, beaten
  3 tablespoons unsalted
      butter or margarine

⅓ cup crumbled almond
   macaroons
¼ cup unsalted shelled
   pistachio nuts, coarsely
   chopped
¼ teaspoon pistachio extract
¼ teaspoon almond extract
Sweetened whipped cream

Prepare the prebaked pie shell; cool completely.

In the top of a double boiler set over simmering water, combine ½ cup of the hot milk with the sugar and flour. Add the remaining milk to the mixture in the double boiler and cook, stirring frequently, for 20 minutes or until thickened. Stir a small amount of the hot custard into the eggs. Combine the egg mixture with the mixture in the double boiler. Cook for 3 minutes more. Remove the pan from the heat. Add the butter, macaroons, pistachio nuts, and pistachio and almond extracts. Turn the filling into the pie shell. Cool, and chill until serving. Serve with sweetened whipped cream.

NO. 164   **JELLY CREAM PIE**

One 9-inch single-crust pie

Pastry for a 9-inch single-crust pie
(Classic Single Crust)
  ½ cup unsalted butter or
     margarine, softened
  2 cups sugar
  2 eggs

½ cup tart jelly
½ cup heavy cream
1 teaspoon vanilla extract

Preheat the oven to 450° F. Prepare the pie pastry. Line the pie pan with the dough. Trim and crimp the edges.

Cream together the butter and sugar. Add the eggs, one at a time, and beat until smooth. Beat in the jelly and the cream. Add the vanilla. Turn the filling into the crust.

Bake at 450° F for 10 minutes. Reduce the heat to 350° F and bake 30 minutes more or until custard is set. Cool, and chill until serving.

NO. 165

MAPLE CREAM PIE

One 9-inch single-crust pie

**Pastry for a 9-inch single-crust pie
(Classic Single Crust)**

2 eggs	1 cup heavy cream
2 tablespoons flour	½ teaspoon tarragon vinegar
½ teaspoon salt	½ cup pecans, coarsely
2 cups maple syrup	chopped

Preheat the oven to 450° F. Prepare the pie pastry. Line the pie pan with the dough. Trim and crimp the edges.

Beat the eggs until light and foamy. Mix in the flour and salt. Add the maple syrup, cream, and vinegar. Stir in the pecans. Turn the filling into the crust.

Bake at 450° F for 10 minutes. Reduce the heat to 325° F and bake 35 to 40 minutes more or until custard is set. Cool, and chill until serving.

NO. 166

MAPLE PRALINE CREAM PIE

One 9-inch single-crust pie

Follow the recipe for Maple Cream Pie (No. 165), adding 1 cup of crushed pecan praline to the filling. Bake as directed.

NO. 167   **MOCHA CREAM PIE**
                                  One 9-inch single-crust pie

Prebaked 9-inch pie shell
(Classic Single Crust)
  3 cups milk, scalded
  ½ cup flour
  ¾ cup sugar
  2 eggs, beaten
  1 teaspoon vanilla extract
  2 tablespoons freshly brewed
    coffee

2 ounces (2 squares)
  unsweetened baking
  chocolate, melted
Sweetened whipped cream

Prepare the prebaked pie shell; cool completely.

In the top of a double boiler set over simmering water, combine ½ cup of the hot milk with the flour and sugar. Add the remaining milk to the mixture in the double boiler, and cook, stirring frequently, for 20 minutes or until thickened. Stir a small amount of the hot custard into the eggs. Combine the egg mixture with the mixture in the double boiler. Cook for 2 minutes more. Remove the pan from the heat. Divide the filling into three parts. To the first part add the vanilla. To the second part add the coffee. To the third part add the melted chocolate. Layer the fillings in the pie shell in the same order; the chocolate layer should be on top. Chill until serving. Serve with sweetened whipped cream.

NO. 168   **OLD ENGLISH CUSTARD PIE**
                                  One 9-inch single-crust pie

Pastry for a 9-inch single-crust pie
(Classic Single Crust)
  ¼ cup pitted prunes,
    coarsely chopped
  ¼ cup dried figs, coarsely
    chopped
  ¼ cup raisins, coarsely
    chopped
  3 tablespoons unsalted
    butter or margarine,
    melted

1 teaspoon cinnamon
¼ teaspoon nutmeg
⅛ teaspoon ground cloves
5 egg yolks, beaten
3 cups milk
½ cup sugar

Preheat the oven to 450° F. Prepare the pie pastry. Line the pie pan with the dough. Trim and crimp the edges.

Mix together the prunes, figs, raisins, butter, cinnamon, nutmeg, and cloves. Arrange the mixture in the bottom of the crust. Combine the egg yolks with the milk and sugar. Mix well. Pour the egg yolk mixture over the fruit mixture.

Bake at 450° F for 10 minutes. Reduce the heat to 325° F and bake 40 minutes more or until the custard is set. Cool, and chill until serving.

NO. 169   **OLD-FASHIONED CREAM PIE**

One 9-inch single-crust pie

Pastry for a 9-inch single-crust pie
(Classic Single Crust)

1½ cups sugar	2 teaspoons vanilla extract
⅓ cup flour	1 tablespoon unsalted butter
2½ cups heavy cream	or margarine, melted

Preheat the oven to 450° F. Prepare the pie pastry. Line the pie pan with the dough. Trim and crimp the edges.

Combine the sugar and flour. Add the cream, vanilla, and melted butter. Mix well. Turn the filling into the crust.

Bake at 450° F for 10 minutes. Reduce the heat to 325° F and bake 45 minutes more. Cool, and chill until serving.

NO. 170   **PEANUT BUTTER CREAM PIE**

One 9-inch single-crust pie

Prebaked 9-inch pie shell
(Classic Single Crust)

2½ cups milk, scalded	2 egg yolks, beaten
½ cup sugar	1 teaspoon vanilla extract
½ cup flour	½ cup peanut butter

Meringue

3 large egg whites, at room temperature	¼ teaspoon cream of tartar
½ teaspoon vanilla extract	6 tablespoons superfine sugar

Prepare the prebaked pie shell; cool completely.

In the top of a double boiler set over simmering water, combine ½ cup of the hot milk with the sugar and flour. Add 1½ cups of hot milk to the mixture in the double boiler and cook, stirring frequently, for 20 minutes or until thickened. Stir a small amount of the hot custard into the egg yolks. Combine the egg yolk mixture with the mixture in the double boiler. Cook for 2 minutes more. Remove the pan from the heat. Add the vanilla. Beat the peanut butter with the remaining milk. Add the peanut butter mixture to the hot custard. Turn the filling into the pie shell.

Preheat the oven to 350° F. While the filling is still hot, prepare the meringue. Beat the egg whites, vanilla, and cream of tartar until the mixture holds stiff peaks. Gradually add the sugar, 1 tablespoon at a time, beating until very stiff and glossy. All the sugar must be dissolved. Spread the meringue over the hot filling, sealing it to the edge of the crust. Bake 12 to 15 minutes or until golden brown. Cool, and chill until serving.

NO. 171   **PECAN CREAM PIE**

One 9-inch single-crust pie

Pastry for a 9-inch single-crust pie
(Classic Single Crust)

2 eggs	1 teaspoon lemon juice
1 cup sugar	¼ teaspoon cinnamon
1 cup heavy cream	¼ teaspoon ground cloves
1 teaspoon flour	1 cup pecans, coarsely
1 teaspoon grated lemon	chopped
zest	Sweetened whipped cream

Preheat the oven to 450° F. Prepare the pie pastry. Line the pie pan with the dough. Trim and crimp the edges.

Beat the eggs until light and thick. Beat in the sugar and cream. Mix in the flour, lemon zest, lemon juice, cinnamon, cloves, and pecans. Turn the filling into the crust.

Bake at 450° F for 10 minutes. Reduce the heat to 350° F and bake 25 to 30 minutes more or until the custard is set. Cool, and chill until serving.

NO. 172   **PINEAPPLE CREAM PIE**

One 9-inch single-crust pie

Prebaked 9-inch pie shell
(Classic Single Crust)

2 cups milk, scalded

¼ cup sugar

¼ cup flour

2 egg yolks, beaten

1 cup coarsely chopped
   canned pineapple,
   drained

2 tablespoons lemon juice

Meringue

3 large egg whites, at room
   temperature

½ teaspoon vanilla extract

¼ teaspoon cream of tartar

6 tablespoons superfine
   sugar

Prepare the prebaked pie shell; cool completely.

In the top of a double boiler set over simmering water, combine ½ cup of the hot milk with the sugar and flour. Add the remaining milk to the mixture in the double boiler and cook, stirring frequently, for 20 minutes or until thickened. Stir a small amount of the hot custard into the egg yolks. Combine the egg yolk mixture with the mixture in the double boiler. Cook for 2 minutes more. Remove the pan from the heat. Add the pineapple and lemon juice. Turn the filling into the pie shell.

Preheat the oven to 350° F. While the filling is still hot, prepare the meringue. Beat the egg whites, vanilla, and cream of tartar until the mixture holds stiff peaks. Gradually add the sugar, 1 tablespoon at a time, beating until very stiff and glossy. All the sugar must be dissolved. Spread the meringue over the hot filling, sealing it to the edge of the crust. Bake 12 to 15 minutes or until golden brown. Cool, and chill until serving.

NO. 173   **PLUM CREAM PIE**

One 9-inch single-crust pie

Follow the recipe for Pineapple Cream Pie (No. 172), substituting 1 cup of peeled, thinly sliced plums for the pineapple and 1 teaspoon of vanilla extract for the lemon juice. Bake as directed.

NO. 174   GOLDEN RAISIN CREAM PIE
                              One 9-inch single-crust pie

Prebaked 9-inch pie shell
(Classic Single Crust)
  1 cup golden raisins   3 tablespoons flour
  2 cups water   2 egg yolks, beaten
  2 cups milk, scalded   ¼ teaspoon lemon extract
  ½ cup dark brown sugar,   2 tablespoons unsalted
    firmly packed   butter or margarine
  2 tablespoons cornstarch   Sweetened whipped cream

Prepare the prebaked pie shell; cool completely.
  Bring the raisins and water to a boil and simmer for 5 minutes.
Drain the raisins and set aside. In the top of a double boiler set
over simmering water, combine ½ cup of the hot milk with the
sugar, cornstarch, and flour. Add the remaining milk to the mixture
in the double boiler and cook, stirring frequently, for 20 minutes
or until thickened. Stir a small amount of the hot custard into the
egg yolks. Combine the egg yolk mixture with the mixture in the
double boiler. Cook for 2 minutes more. Remove the pan from
the heat. Add the lemon extract and butter. Stir in the raisins.
Turn the filling into the pie shell. Cool, and chill until serving.
Serve with sweetened whipped cream.

NO. 175 GOLDEN RAISIN WALNUT CREAM
PIE

One 9-inch single-crust pie

Follow the recipe for Golden Raisin Cream Pie (No. 174), adding
½ cup of coarsely chopped walnuts to the hot custard. Omit the
meringue and serve cool, with sweetened whipped cream.

NO. 176 RAISIN MERINGUE PIE

One 9-inch single-crust pie

Prebaked 9-inch pie shell
(Classic Single Crust)

1 cup sugar
4 tablespoons cornstarch
1 tablespoon unsalted butter
  or margarine
2 cups boiling water
4 tablespoons orange juice

1 teaspoon grated orange
  zest
1½ cups raisins, coarsely
  chopped
3 egg yolks, beaten

Meringue

3 large egg whites, at room
  temperature
½ teaspoon vanilla extract

¼ teaspoon cream of tartar
6 tablespoons superfine
  sugar

Prepare the prebaked pie shell; cool completely.

In the top of a double boiler set over simmering water, combine
the sugar, cornstarch, and butter. Mix well. Stir in the boiling
water, a little at a time. Cook, stirring constantly, for 5 minutes.
Add the orange juice, orange zest, and raisins. Bring the mixture
to a boil. Stir a small portion of the raisin mixture into the egg
yolks. Combine the egg yolk mixture with the mixture in the
double boiler. Cook for 2 minutes more. Remove the pan from
the heat. Turn the filling into the pie shell.

While the filling is still hot, prepare the meringue. Preheat the
oven to 350° F. Beat the egg whites, vanilla, and cream of tartar
until the mixture holds stiff peaks. Gradually add the sugar, 1
tablespoon at a time, beating until very stiff and glossy. All the
sugar must be dissolved. Spread the meringue over the hot filling,
sealing it to the edge of the crust. Bake 12 to 15 minutes or until
golden brown. Cool, and chill until serving.

NO. 177   **RHUBARB CUSTARD PIE**
                                    One 9-inch lattice-top pie

Pastry for a 9-inch lattice-top pie
(Classic Double Crust)

1 cup light brown sugar, firmly packed	3 cups diced fresh rhubarb
3 tablespoons flour	1 tablespoon sugar
2 eggs, beaten	

Preheat the oven to 450° F. Prepare the pie pastry. Line the pie pan with the bottom crust, using half of the dough. Keep the remaining dough chilled.

Combine the sugar with 2 tablespoons of the flour. Mix in the eggs and rhubarb. Sprinkle the remaining flour in the bottom of the crust. Turn the filling into the crust. Roll out, cut, and lay on the lattice strips. After the pie is latticed and crimped, sprinkle 1 tablespoon of sugar over the lattice crust.

Bake at 450° F for 10 minutes. Reduce the heat to 350° F and bake about 30 minutes more or until the custard is set. Cool, and chill until serving.

NO. 178   **SOUR CREAM BUTTERSCOTCH PIE**
                                    One 9-inch single-crust pie

Pastry for a 9-inch single-crust pie
(Classic Single Crust)

1 tablespoon flour	2 egg yolks, beaten
1 cup dark brown sugar, firmly packed	1 teaspoon vanilla extract
¼ teaspoon salt	1 tablespoon unsalted butter or margarine, melted
1 cup sour cream	

Meringue

3 large egg whites, at room temperature	¼ teaspoon cream of tartar
½ teaspoon vanilla extract	6 tablespoons superfine sugar

Preheat the oven to 450° F. Prepare the pie pastry. Line the pie pan with the dough. Trim and crimp the edges.

Combine the flour, sugar, salt, sour cream, egg yolks, vanilla, and butter. Mix well. Turn the filling into the crust.

Bake at 450° F for 10 minutes. Reduce the heat to 350° F and bake 45 minutes more or until the custard is set. Remove the pie from the oven and prepare the meringue.

While the filling is still hot, beat the egg whites, vanilla, and cream of tartar until the mixture holds stiff peaks. Gradually add the sugar, 1 tablespoon at a time, beating until very stiff and glossy. All the sugar must be dissolved. Spread the meringue over the pie filling, sealing it to the edge of the crust. Bake 12 to 15 minutes or until golden brown. Cool, and chill until serving.

NO. 179   # STRAWBERRY CREAM PIE

One 9-inch single-crust pie

Prebaked 9-inch pie shell
(Classic Single Crust)

1½ cups milk, scalded	2 egg yolks, beaten
½ cup sugar	1 teaspoon vanilla extract
6 tablespoons flour	1½ cups sliced fresh strawberries

Meringue

3 large egg whites, at room temperature	¼ teaspoon cream of tartar
½ teaspoon vanilla extract	6 tablespoons superfine sugar

Prepare the prebaked pie shell; cool completely.

In the top of a double boiler set over simmering water, combine ½ cup of the hot milk with the sugar and flour. Add the remaining milk to the mixture in the double boiler and cook, stirring frequently, for 20 minutes or until thickened. Stir a small amount of the hot custard into the egg yolks. Combine the egg yolk mixture with the mixture in the double boiler. Cook for 2 minutes more. Remove the pan from the heat. Add the vanilla. Turn the filling into the pie shell. Arrange the strawberries on top of the filling.

Preheat the oven to 350° F. While the filling is still hot, prepare the meringue. Beat the egg whites, vanilla, and cream of tartar until the mixture holds stiff peaks. Gradually add the sugar, 1 tablespoon at a time, beating until very stiff and glossy. All the sugar must be dissolved. Spread the meringue over the hot filling, sealing it to the edge of the crust. Bake 12 to 15 minutes or until golden brown. Cool, and chill until serving.

NO. **180**   **VANILLA CREAM PIE**
                                 One 9-inch single-crust pie

Follow the recipe for Strawberry Cream Pie (No. 179), omitting
the strawberries. Bake as directed.

NO. **181**   **VANILLA CUSTARD PIE**
                                 One 9-inch single-crust pie

Pastry for a 9-inch single-crust pie
(Classic Single Crust)

  4 eggs, beaten   2 teaspoons vanilla extract
  ½ cup sugar   ¼ teaspoon nutmeg
  3 cups milk

Preheat the oven to 450° F. Prepare the pie pastry. Line the pie
pan with the dough. Trim and crimp the edges.
    Beat the eggs with the sugar and milk. Add the vanilla. Turn
the filling into the crust and sprinkle the nutmeg over the top.
    Bake at 450° F for 10 minutes. Reduce the heat to 325° F and
bake 25 to 30 minutes more or until the custard is set. Cool, and
chill until serving.

NO. **182**   **WALNUT CUSTARD PIE**
                                 One 9-inch single-crust pie

Follow the recipe for Vanilla Custard Pie (No. 181), adding 1 cup
of coarsely chopped walnuts to the filling. Bake as directed.

NO. **183**   **HAZELNUT CUSTARD PIE**
                                 One 9-inch single-crust pie

Follow the recipe for Vanilla Custard Pie (No. 181), adding 1 cup
of ground hazelnuts to the filling. Bake as directed.

NO. 184   **VERMONT CREAM PIE**

One 9-inch single-crust pie

Pastry for a 9-inch single-crust pie
(Classic Single Crust)

4 egg whites	2 cups heavy cream
1 tablespoon flour	1 teaspoon vanilla extract
½ cup shaved maple sugar	¼ teaspoon nutmeg

Preheat the oven to 450° F. Prepare the pie pastry. Line the pie pan with the dough. Trim and crimp the edges.

Beat the egg whites until they hold stiff peaks. Mix together the flour and sugar. Fold the egg whites into the flour mixture. Heat the cream, and stir into the flour mixture. Add the vanilla and nutmeg. Turn the filling into the crust.

Bake at 450° F for 10 minutes. Reduce the heat to 325° F and bake 30 to 35 minutes more or until the custard is set. Cool, and chill until serving.

Chiffon and Other Gelatin Pies

A perfectly fluffy chiffon pie is a deliciously harmonious balance of sweet filling and beaten egg white. Rich black bottom pie, made with chocolate and rum, is well-represented here in two enticing recipes. Other classics include chocolate chiffon, strawberry chiffon, and Nesselrode pies, as well as daiquiri pie and a peanut butter chiffon pie. A graham cracker or vanilla wafer crust is a quick, easy alternate to a standard prebaked pie shell and goes particularly well with a chiffon filling. To set properly, chiffon pies should chill for at least 2 hours before serving; be sure there is sufficient time for cooling.

APPLE BUTTER CHIFFON PIE

One 9-inch single-crust pie

Prebaked 9-inch pie shell
(Classic Single Crust or Graham Cracker Crust)

1 envelope unflavored gelatin	½ cup milk
1½ cups cold water	1½ teaspoons cinnamon
3 eggs, separated	½ teaspoon nutmeg
½ cup dark brown sugar, firmly packed	⅛ teaspoon cloves
½ cup apple butter	2 tablespoons sugar
	Sweetened whipped cream

Prepare the prebaked pie shell; cool completely.

Mix the gelatin with ½ cup of the water. Set aside. Beat the egg yolks. In the top of a double boiler set over simmering water, combine the egg yolks, brown sugar, apple butter, milk, the remaining water, cinnamon, nutmeg, and cloves. Cook, stirring frequently, until thickened. Stir in the gelatin mixture until completely dissolved. Remove the pan from the heat. Chill until slightly thickened. Beat the egg whites until they form stiff peaks. Beat the sugar into the egg whites. Fold the egg white mixture into the custard. Turn the filling into the pie shell. Chill until set. Serve with sweetened whipped cream.

APRICOT ORANGE GELATIN PIE

One 9-inch single-crust pie

Prebaked 9-inch pie shell
(Graham Cracker Crust)

2 cups dried apricot halves	1 tablespoon apricot liqueur
2 cups water	Sweetened whipped cream
1 package orange gelatin mix	

Prepare the prebaked pie shell; cool completely.

Combine the apricots and water in a saucepan. Bring the mixture to a boil. Remove the pan from the heat. Drain the apricots, reserving the liquid. Return the liquid to the stove and bring to a boil. Remove the pan from the heat. Add the gelatin mix, stirring until completely dissolved. Stir in the apricot liqueur. Arrange the apricots over the bottom of the pie shell. Pour the gelatin mixture over the apricots. Chill until set. Serve with sweetened whipped cream.

NO. 187   **PEAR STRAWBERRY GELATIN PIE**

One 9-inch single-crust pie

Follow the recipe for Apricot Orange Gelatin Pie (No. 186), substituting dried pears for dried apricots and strawberry gelatin mix for orange gelatin mix.

NO. 188   **BLACK BOTTOM PIE I**

One 9-inch single-crust pie

Prebaked 9-inch pie shell
(Classic Single Crust)

1 envelope unflavored gelatin	2 ounces (2 squares) unsweetened baking chocolate, melted
¼ cup cold water	1 teaspoon vanilla extract
1 cup sugar	⅛ teaspoon cream of tartar
1½ tablespoons cornstarch	1 tablespoon rum
2 eggs, separated	Sweetened whipped cream
1¾ cups milk, scalded	Chocolate shavings

Prepare the prebaked pie shell; cool completely.

Mix the gelatin with the water. Set aside. In the top of a double boiler set over simmering water, combine ¾ cup of the sugar with the cornstarch. Beat the egg yolks and add to the sugar mixture. Slowly add the hot milk, stirring constantly. Cook, stirring frequently, for about 20 minutes or until thickened. Remove the pan from the heat. Stir in the gelatin mixture until completely dissolved. Divide the custard in half. To one half add the melted chocolate and vanilla. Turn the chocolate custard into the bottom of the pie shell. Beat the egg whites until they form stiff peaks. Beat in the remaining sugar and cream of tartar. Fold the egg white mixture into the remaining custard. Add the rum. Spread the rum custard over the chocolate custard. Chill until set. Serve with sweetened whipped cream and chocolate shavings.

NO. 189   **BLACK BOTTOM PIE II**
One 9-inch single-crust pie

Prebaked 9-inch pie shell
(Gingersnap Crust)
  1 envelope unflavored   2 ounces (2 squares)
    gelatin   unsweetened baking
  ¼ cup cold water   chocolate, melted
  2 cups milk, scalded   2 teaspoons vanilla extract
  1 cup sugar   ¼ teaspoon cream of tartar
1½ tablespoons cornstarch   2 tablespoons rum
  4 eggs, separated   Sweetened whipped cream
                                  Chocolate shavings

Prepare the prebaked pie shell; cool completely.

Mix the gelatin with the water. Set aside. In the top of a double boiler set over simmering water, combine ½ cup of the sugar and the cornstarch. Beat the egg yolks and stir into the sugar mixture. Slowly add the hot milk to the sugar mixture, stirring constantly. Cook, stirring frequently, for about 20 minutes or until thickened. Remove the pan from the heat. Stir in the gelatin mixture until completely dissolved. Divide the custard in half. To one half add the melted chocolate and vanilla. Turn the chocolate custard into the bottom of the pie shell. Beat the egg whites until they form stiff peaks. Beat in the remaining sugar and cream of tartar. Fold the egg white mixture into the remaining custard. Add the rum. Spread the rum custard over the chocolate custard. Chill until set. Serve with sweetened whipped cream and chocolate shavings.

NO. 190   **BUTTERSCOTCH CHIFFON PIE**
One 9-inch single-crust pie

Prebaked 9-inch pie shell
(Gingersnap Crust)

1 envelope unflavored   ½ cup milk
  gelatin   1 teaspoon grated orange
¼ cup cold water   zest
½ cup dark brown sugar,   1 teaspoon vanilla extract
  firmly packed   ¼ cup sugar
1 tablespoon unsalted butter   Sweetened whipped cream
  or margarine
¼ cup hot water
3 eggs, separated

Prepare the prebaked pie shell; cool completely.

Mix together the gelatin and cold water. Set aside. In a saucepan, combine the brown sugar and butter. Cook over very low heat, stirringly constantly, for about 5 minutes. Remove the pan from the heat and cool. When the mixture is no longer bubbling, carefully add the hot water. Cook over low heat, stirring constantly, until the caramelized sugar is completely dissolved. Beat the egg yolks. In the top of a double boiler set over simmering water, combine the egg yolks, milk, caramel syrup, and orange zest. Cook, stirring frequently, for 20 minutes or until thickened. Remove the pan from the heat. Stir in the gelatin mixture and vanilla. Cool until slightly thickened. Beat the egg whites until they form stiff peaks. Beat the sugar into the egg whites, a little at a time. Fold the custard into the egg white mixture. Turn the filling into the pie shell. Chill until set. Serve with sweetened whipped cream.

NO. 191   **CARAMEL WALNUT CHIFFON PIE**
One 9-inch single-crust pie

Follow the recipe for Butterscotch Chiffon Pie (No. 190), adding ½ cup of chopped walnuts to the cooled custard.

NO. 192   **CHERRY PEACH GELATIN PIE**

One 9-inch single-crust pie

Prebaked 9-inch pie shell
(Graham Cracker Crust)

2 cups water
1 package cherry gelatin mix
¼ cup sugar
2 tablespoons lemon juice

2½ cups halved, pitted fresh
   sweet cherries
1 cup sliced peaches
Sweetened whipped cream

Prepare the prebaked pie shell; cool completely.

Bring the water to a boil. Remove the pan from the heat. Add the gelatin mix, sugar, and lemon juice. Stir until completely dissolved. Divide the gelatin in half. Chill one half until slightly thickened. Place the gelatin over a bowl of crushed ice or ice water and beat until fluffy and thick. Fold in ½ cup of the cherries. Turn the fluffy gelatin mixture into the pie shell. Arrange the remaining peaches and cherries on top. Pour on the remaining gelatin and chill until set. Serve with sweetened whipped cream.

NO. 193   **CHOCOLATE CHIFFON PIE**

One 9-inch single-crust pie

Prebaked 9-inch pie shell
(Classic Single Crust)

1 envelope unflavored
   gelatin
¼ cup cold water
½ cup boiling water
2 ounces (2 squares)
   unsweetened baking
   chocolate, melted

4 eggs, separated
1 cup sugar
1 teaspoon vanilla extract

Prepare the prebaked pie shell; cool completely.

Mix together the gelatin and cold water. Set aside. Combine the boiling water and melted chocolate. Mix well. Add the gelatin mixture to the chocolate mixture. Cool until slightly thickened. Beat the egg yolks with ½ cup of the sugar and the vanilla. Stir the egg yolk mixture into the chocolate mixture. Cool. Beat the egg whites with the remaining sugar. Fold the egg white mixture into the custard. Turn the filling into the pie shell. Chill until set. Serve with sweetened whipped cream.

NO. 194   **COFFEE CHIFFON PIE**

One 9-inch single-crust pie

Prebaked 9-inch pie shell
(Classic Single Crust or Graham Cracker Crust)

1 envelope unflavored gelatin	3 eggs, separated
1 cup black coffee	1 teaspoon vanilla extract
¾ cup sugar	Sweetened whipped cream
½ teaspoon cinnamon	

Prepare the prebaked pie shell; cool completely.

Mix the gelatin with 2 tablespoons of the coffee. Combine the gelatin mixture with the sugar, cinnamon, and egg yolks. Bring the remaining coffee to a boil. Slowly stir the coffee into the gelatin mixture. In the top of a double boiler set over simmering water, cook until slightly thickened. Remove the pan from the heat. Chill for 15 minutes, then beat until light and foamy. Beat the egg whites until they form stiff peaks. Fold the egg whites into the custard. Add the vanilla. Turn the filling into the pie shell.

Chill until set. Serve with sweetened whipped cream.

NO. 195   **CRANBERRY CHIFFON PIE**

One 9-inch single-crust pie

Prebaked 9-inch pie shell
(Vanilla Wafer Crust)

1 envelope unflavored gelatin	½ cup apricot nectar
1½ cups unsweetened cranberry juice	1 teaspoon grated orange zest
¾ cup sugar	3 egg whites
¼ cup flour	½ cup heavy cream

Prepare the prebaked pie shell; cool completely.

Mix together the gelatin and ¼ cup of the cranberry juice. Stir until completely dissolved. Set aside. In the top of a double boiler set over simmering water, combine ½ cup of the sugar, flour, remaining cranberry juice, orange zest, and apricot nectar. Cook, stirring frequently, until thickened. Remove from heat. Stir in the gelatin mixture until completely dissolved. Cool to room temperature then chill for 45 minutes. Beat the egg whites until they form stiff peaks. Beat the remaining sugar into the egg whites, a little at a time. Fold the egg white mixture into the custard. Whip the cream, and fold into the custard. Turn the filling into the pie shell. Chill until set.

NO. 196   **EGGNOG CHIFFON PIE**

One 9-inch single-crust pie

Prebaked 9-inch pie shell
(Classic Single Crust or Gingersnap Crust)

3 eggs, separated	1 envelope unflavored
1¾ cups heavy cream	gelatin
½ cup sugar	2 tablespoons milk
¼ teaspoon nutmeg	⅛ cup dark rum
	1 teaspoon vanilla extract

Prepare the prebaked pie shell; cool completely.

Beat the egg yolks. In the top of a double boiler set over simmering water, combine the egg yolks, 1 cup of the cream, sugar, and nutmeg. Cook, stirring constantly, until slightly thickened. Combine the gelatin with the milk. Add the gelatin mixture to the custard. Remove the pan from the heat. Stir in the rum and vanilla. Chill until slightly thickened. Beat the egg whites until they form stiff peaks. Fold the egg whites into the custard. Whip the remaining cream and mix into the custard. Turn the filling into the pie shell. Chill until set.

NO. 197   **LEMON CHIFFON PIE**

One 9-inch single-crust pie

Prebaked 9-inch pie shell
(Classic Single Crust or Graham Cracker Crust)

1 envelope unflavored	½ cup lemon juice
gelatin	2 teaspoons grated lemon
¼ cup cold water	zest
4 eggs, separated	Sweetened whipped cream
1 cup sugar	

Prepare the prebaked pie shell; cool completely.

Mix together the gelatin and water. Beat the egg yolks. In the top of a double boiler set over simmering water, combine the egg yolks, ½ cup of the sugar, lemon juice, and lemon zest. Mix well.

Cook, stirring frequently, until thickened. Remove the pan from the heat. Stir in the gelatin mixture until completely dissolved. Chill until slightly thickened. Beat the egg whites until they form stiff peaks. Beat in the remaining sugar, a little at a time. Fold the egg white mixture into the custard. Turn the filling into the pie shell. Chill until set. Serve with sweetened whipped cream.

NO. 198 **LEMON ORANGE CHIFFON PIE**

One 9-inch single-crust pie

Follow the recipe for Lemon Chiffon Pie (No. 197), substituting for ½ cup of lemon juice, ¼ cup of lemon juice plus ¼ cup of orange juice. Add 1 teaspoon of grated orange zest together with the lemon zest.

NO. 199 **LEMON LIME CHIFFON PIE**

One 9-inch single-crust pie

Follow the recipe for Lemon Chiffon Pie (No. 197), substituting for ½ cup of lemon juice, approximately ¼ cup of lemon juice plus ¼ cup of lime juice. Add 1 teaspoon of grated lime zest together with the lemon zest.

NO. 200 **LIME CHIFFON PIE**

One 9-inch single-crust pie

Prebaked 9-inch pie shell
(Graham Cracker Crust)
  2 **envelopes unflavored**
    gelatin
  ½ **cup cold water**
  3 **eggs, separated**
  1 **cup sugar**

½ **cup lime juice**
2 **teaspoons grated lime zest**
Sweetened whipped cream

Prepare the prebaked pie shell; cool completely.

Mix together the gelatin and water. Set aside. Beat the egg yolks. In the top of a double boiler set over simmering water, combine the egg yolks and ½ cup of the sugar. Cook, stirring constantly, until hot. Stir in the gelatin mixture until completely dissolved. Remove the pan from the heat. Mix in the lime juice and 1½ teaspoons of the lime zest. Cool to room temperature. Beat the egg whites until they form stiff peaks. Beat the remaining sugar into the egg whites, a little at a time. Beat in the remaining lime zest. Fold the egg white mixture into the custard. Turn the filling into the pie shell. Chill until set. Serve with sweetened whipped cream.

NO. 201

DAIQUIRI PIE

One 9-inch single-crust pie

Follow the recipe for Lime Chiffon Pie (No. 200), adding ½ cup of dark rum to the hot custard.

NO. 202

MOLASSES CHIFFON PIE

One 9-inch single-crust pie

Prebaked 9-inch pie shell
(Graham Cracker Crust)

1 envelope unflavored gelatin	⅔ cup milk
3 tablespoons cold water	¼ teaspoon baking soda
2 eggs, separated	1½ tablespoons lemon juice
⅓ cup dark molasses	

Topping

1 ounce (1 square) unsweetened baking chocolate	½ cup sugar
¼ cup milk	½ cup heavy cream

Prepare the prebaked pie shell; cool completely.

Mix together the gelatin and water. Set aside. Beat the egg yolks. In the top of a double boiler set over simmering water, combine the egg yolks, molasses, milk, and baking soda. Cook, stirring frequently, for 10 minutes. Remove the pan from the heat. Stir in the gelatin mixture and lemon juice. Chill until slightly thickened. Beat the egg whites until they form stiff peaks. Fold the egg whites into the custard. Turn the filling into the pie shell. Chill until set.

To prepare the topping, in the top of a double boiler set over simmering water, melt the chocolate. Add the milk and sugar. Cook, stirring constantly, until smooth. Remove the pan from the heat and cool the mixture. Whip the cream. Fold the whipped cream into the chocolate mixture. Spread the chocolate cream on top of the set custard. Refrigerate until ready to serve.

NO. 203   ## NESSELRODE PIE

One 9-inch single-crust pie

Prebaked 9-inch pie shell
(Classic Single Crust or Graham Cracker Crust)

1 envelope unflavored gelatin	⅛ teaspoon nutmeg
¼ cup cold water	¼ cup plus 6 tablespoons sugar
1 cup heavy cream	2 teaspoons rum
1 cup milk	Chocolate shavings
2 eggs, separated	

Prepare the prebaked pie shell; cool completely.

Mix together the gelatin and water. Set aside. In the top of a double boiler set over simmering water, combine the milk and cream. Scald the mixture. Beat the egg yolks until foamy. Mix one quarter cup of the sugar into the egg yolks. Slowly add the hot cream mixture to the egg yolk mixture, stirring constantly. Return the custard to the double boiler. Cook, stirring constantly, for 5 minutes, until thickened. Remove the pan from the heat. Stir in the gelatin mixture and the rum. Chill until slightly thickened. Beat the egg whites until they form stiff peaks. Gradually beat the remaining sugar into the egg whites. Fold the egg white mixture into the custard. Turn the filling into the pie shell. Chill until set. To serve, decorate with chocolate shavings.

NO. 204 **ORANGE CHIFFON PIE**
One 9-inch single-crust pie

Prebaked 9-inch pie shell
(Classic Single Crust or Graham Cracker Crust)

1 envelope unflavored
   gelatin
¼ cup cold water
4 eggs, separated
1 cup sugar

½ cup orange juice
1 tablespoon lemon juice
1 tablespoon grated orange
   zest
Sweetened whipped cream

Prepare the prebaked pie shell; cool completely.

Mix together the gelatin and water. Set aside. Beat the egg yolks. In the top of a double boiler set over simmering water, combine the egg yolks, ½ cup of the sugar, orange juice, and lemon juice. Cook, stirring frequently, until thickened. Stir in the gelatin mixture until completely dissolved. Add the orange zest. Remove the pan from the heat. Chill until slightly thickened. Beat the egg whites until they form stiff peaks. Beat the remaining sugar into the egg whites, a little at a time. Fold the egg white mixture into the custard. Turn the filling into the pie shell. Chill until set. Serve with sweetened whipped cream.

NO. 205 **PEANUT BUTTER CHIFFON PIE**
One 9-inch single-crust pie

Prebaked 9-inch pie shell
(Classic Single Crust or Graham Cracker Crust)

2 envelopes unflavored
   gelatin
1 cup cold water
2 eggs, separated
¼ cup sugar

½ cup peanut butter
1 teaspoon vanilla extract
Sweetened whipped cream

Prepare the prebaked pie shell; cool completely.

Mix the gelatin with ¼ cup of the water. Set aside. Beat the egg yolks. In the top of a double boiler set over simmering water, combine the egg yolks, ⅛ cup of the sugar, and ¼ cup of the water. Mix well. Stir in the gelatin mixture until completely dissolved. Cook, stirring constantly, for 5 minutes. Remove the pan from the heat and cool. Combine the peanut butter, the remaining water, and the vanilla. Beat until smooth. Beat in the egg mixture. Chill until slightly thickened. Beat the egg whites until they form stiff peaks. Beat the remaining sugar into the egg whites, a little at a time. Gently fold the egg white mixture into the custard. Turn the filling into the pie shell. Chill until set. Serve with sweetened whipped cream.

NO. 206   **PEANUT BRITTLE CHIFFON PIE**
                                        One 9-inch single-crust pie

Follow the recipe for Peanut Butter Chiffon Pie (No. 205), adding ½ cup of crushed peanut brittle to the custard.

NO. 207   **PINEAPPLE CHIFFON PIE**
                                        One 9-inch single-crust pie

Prebaked 9-inch pie shell
(Classic Single Crust or Graham Cracker Crust)

4 eggs, separated	¼ cup lemon juice
1¼ cups sugar	½ cup pineapple juice
¼ cup canned crushed pineapple, drained	1 envelope unflavored gelatin
1 teaspoon grated lemon zest	Sweetened whipped cream

Prepare the prebaked pie shell; cool completely.

Beat the egg yolks. In the top of a double boiler set over simmering water, combine the egg yolks, ½ cup of the sugar, pineapple, and lemon zest. Cook, stirring frequently, until the mixture coats the back of a spoon. In a separate saucepan, bring the lemon and pineapple juices to a boil. Add the gelatin and stir until dissolved. Blend the gelatin mixture into the hot custard. Remove the pan from the heat and cool to room temperature. Beat the egg whites until they form stiff peaks. Beat the remaining sugar into the egg whites, a little at a time. Fold the egg white mixture into the custard. Turn the filling into the pie shell. Chill until set. Serve with sweetened whipped cream.

NO. 208

SEAFOAM CHIFFON PIE

One 9-inch single-crust pie

Prebaked 9-inch pie shell
(Graham Cracker Crust)
  1 envelope unflavored
     gelatin
  ¼ cup cold water
1½ cups sugar
  2 tablespoons flour

¾ cup lime juice
  Green food coloring
3 egg whites

Prepare the prebaked pie shell; cool completely.

Mix together the gelatin and water. Set aside. Combine 1 cup of the sugar with the flour. In the top of a double boiler set over simmering water, combine the sugar mixture and lime juice. Cook, stirring frequently, for 20 minutes. Stir in the gelatin mixture until completely dissolved. Remove the pan from the heat. Add the food coloring, a drop at a time, until the mixture is deep green. Chill until slightly thickened. Beat the egg whites until they form stiff peaks. Beat the remaining sugar into the egg whites. Fold the egg white mixture into the custard. Turn the filling into the pie shell. Using the back of a spoon, make "waves" in the surface of the pie. Chill until set.

NO. 209

STRAWBERRY CHIFFON PIE

One 9-inch single-crust pie

Prebaked 9-inch pie shell
(Classic Single Crust or Graham Cracker Crust)
  2 cups sliced fresh
     strawberries
  ½ cup sugar
  1 envelope unflavored
     gelatin
  ¼ cup cold water
  ½ cup strawberry juice

1 tablespoon orange juice
½ cup heavy cream
3 egg whites
  Sweetened whipped cream

Prepare the prebaked pie shell; cool completely.

Mix the strawberries with the sugar and let stand for 30 minutes. Combine the gelatin with the water. Set aside. In the top of a double boiler set over simmering water, bring the strawberry and orange juices to a boil. Add the gelatin mixture. Remove the pan from the heat. Stir in the strawberry mixture. Chill until slightly thickened. Whip the cream and fold into the gelatin mixture. Beat the egg whites until they form stiff peaks. Fold the egg white mixture into the gelatin mixture. Turn the filling into the pie shell. Chill until set. Serve with sweetened whipped cream.

NO. 210   **BLUEBERRY CHIFFON PIE**
One 9-inch single-crust pie

Follow the recipe for Strawberry Chiffon Pie (No. 209), substituting blueberries for strawberries and cherry juice for strawberry juice.

NO. 211   **RASPBERRY CHIFFON PIE**
One 9-inch single-crust pie

Follow the recipe for Strawberry Chiffon Pie (No. 209), substituting raspberries for strawberries and raspberry juice for strawberry juice.

NO. 212   **PEACH CHIFFON PIE**
One 9-inch single-crust pie

Follow the recipe for Strawberry Chiffon Pie (No. 209), substituting peaches for strawberries and peach or apricot nectar for strawberry juice.

NO. 213 **WALNUT CUSTARD CHIFFON PIE**

One 9-inch single-crust pie

Prebaked 9-inch pie shell
(Classic Single Crust or Graham Cracker Crust)

1 envelope unflavored gelatin	1 tablespoon rum
¼ cup cold water	¼ teaspoon nutmeg
2 eggs, separated	1 cup ground walnuts
2 cups milk	Sweetened whipped cream
½ cup sugar	Chocolate shavings
2 tablespoons flour	

Prepare the prebaked pie shell; cool completely.

Mix together the gelatin and water. Beat the egg yolks with ½ cup of the milk. Stir the sugar and flour into the egg yolk mixture. In the top of a double boiler set over simmering water, scald the remaining milk. Pour a small amount of the hot milk into the egg yolk mixture. Stir, and add the remaining milk. Return the mixture to the double boiler. Cook, stirring frequently, for 20 minutes or until thickened. Remove the pan from the heat. Stir in the gelatin mixture until completely dissolved. Chill until thickened. Add the rum, nutmeg, and walnuts. Beat the egg whites until they form stiff peaks. Fold the egg white mixture into the custard. Turn the filling into the pie shell. Chill until set. Serve with sweetened whipped cream and sprinkle with chocolate.

NO. 214 **HAZELNUT CUSTARD CHIFFON PIE**

One 9-inch single-crust pie

Follow the recipe for Walnut Custard Chiffon Pie (No. 213), substituting ground hazelnuts for ground walnuts.

NO. 215 **PECAN CUSTARD CHIFFON PIE**

One 9-inch single-crust pie

Follow the recipe for Walnut Custard Chiffon Pie (No. 213), substituting ground pecans for ground walnuts.

Sweet Vegetable Pies

No Thanksgiving feast is complete without a rich pumpkin pie, and a green tomato pie is the eager gardener's reward for the first, early harvest. Sweet vegetable pies have found a warm welcome on tables everywhere—from the very first pioneer squash to the present day. Pumpkin pie enthusiasts looking for something special will find twelve unique recipes for pumpkin pie as well as many other savory tributes to the virtues of the sweet potato, squash, and green tomato.

GREEN TOMATO PIE I

One 9-inch double-crust pie

Pastry for a 9-inch double-crust pie
(Classic Double Crust)

1 cup light brown sugar, firmly packed
1 teaspoon cinnamon
3 tablespoons flour

3 cups very thinly sliced green tomatoes
2 whole thin-skinned lemons, thinly sliced
2 tablespoons unsalted butter or margarine

Preheat the oven to 425° F. Prepare the pie pastry. Line the pie pan with the bottom crust, using half of the dough. Keep the remaining dough chilled.

Combine the sugar, cinnamon, and flour. Arrange a layer of tomatoes over the bottom of the crust. Cover with a layer of lemon slices and sprinkle with some of the sugar mixture. Continue to layer the ingredients until the pie is filled. Dot with butter. Roll out the top crust and lay it on the filling. Trim off any excess dough, crimp the edges, and prick with the tines of a fork to vent.

Bake at 425° F for 10 minutes. Reduce the heat to 350° F and bake 25 minutes more or until golden brown.

GREEN TOMATO PIE II

One 9-inch double-crust pie

Pastry for a 9-inch double-crust pie
(Classic Double Crust)

2 tablespoons flour
1 cup sugar
½ teaspoon cinnamon
¼ teaspoon ground ginger

3 cups very thinly sliced green tomatoes
2 tablespoons unsalted butter or margarine
1 tablespoon vinegar

Preheat the oven to 450° F. Prepare the pie pastry. Line the pie pan with the bottom crust, using half of the dough. Keep the remaining dough chilled.

Mix together the flour, sugar, cinnamon, and ginger. Sprinkle one fourth of the flour mixture in the bottom of the pie shell. Arrange the tomato slices in the crust. Cover with the remaining flour mixture. Dot with butter and sprinkle with vinegar. Roll out the top crust and lay it on the filling. Trim off any excess dough, crimp the edges, and prick with the tines of a fork to vent.

Bake at 450° F for 10 minutes. Reduce the heat to 350° F and bake 50 minutes more or until golden brown.

NO. 218   **GREEN TOMATO PIE III**
                                    One 9-inch double-crust pie

**Pastry for a 9-inch double-crust pie
(Classic Double Crust)**

1 cup dark brown sugar, firmly packed	2 cups very thinly sliced green tomatoes
2 tablespoons flour	2 cups peeled, cored, and thinly sliced apples
1 teaspoon cinnamon	2 tablespoons unsalted butter or margarine
¼ teaspoon nutmeg	

Preheat the oven to 450° F. Prepare the pie pastry. Line the pie pan with the bottom crust, using half of the dough. Keep the remaining dough chilled.

Combine the sugar, flour, cinnamon, and nutmeg. Sprinkle one third of the sugar mixture in the bottom of the pie shell. Mix the tomatoes with the apples. Layer one half of the tomato mixture in the pie shell. Sprinkle with another third of the sugar mixture. Make an additional layer of tomatoes and apples and top with the remaining sugar mixture. Dot with butter. Roll out the top crust and lay it on the filling. Trim off any excess dough, crimp the edges, and prick with the tines of a fork to vent.

Bake at 450° F for 15 minutes. Reduce the heat to 350° F and bake for 30 minutes or until golden brown.

NO. 219   **CLASSIC PUMPKIN PIE**

One 9-inch single-crust pie

Prebaked 9-inch pie shell
(Classic Single Crust)

- 1 cup dark brown sugar, firmly packed
- 4 tablespoons flour
- 1 teaspoon cinnamon
- ¼ teaspoon ground cloves
- ½ teaspoon ground ginger
- ¼ teaspoon nutmeg
- ½ teaspoon salt
- 3 egg yolks, beaten
- 1 cup milk
- 1 cup canned pumpkin purée
- ¼ cup unsalted butter or margarine, melted
- Vanilla ice cream

Prepare the prebaked pie shell; cool completely.

Preheat the oven to 350° F. Mix together the sugar, flour, cinnamon, cloves, ginger, nutmeg, and salt. In the top of a double boiler set over simmering water, combine the egg yolks and milk. Stir in the sugar mixture. Cook, stirring constantly, until thickened. Mix in the pumpkin and butter. Remove the pan from the heat. Turn the filling into the crust.

Bake 12 to 15 minutes. Serve with vanilla ice cream.

NO. 220   **PUMPKIN MERINGUE PIE**

One 9-inch single-crust pie

Recipe for Classic Pumpkin Pie (No. 219)

Meringue

- 3 large egg whites, at room temperature
- ½ teaspoon vanilla extract
- ¼ teaspoon cream of tartar
- 6 tablespoons superfine sugar

Prepare the recipe for Classic Pumpkin Pie. Bake as directed.

While the pie is still hot, prepare the meringue. Preheat the oven to 350° F. Beat the egg whites, vanilla, and cream of tartar until the mixture holds stiff peaks. Gradually add the sugar, 1 tablespoon at a time, beating until very stiff and glossy. All the sugar must be dissolved. Spread the meringue over the pie filling, sealing it to the edge of the crust. Bake 12 to 15 minutes or until golden brown. Cool before serving.

NO. 221   **PUMPKIN PECAN PIE**
                          One 9-inch single-crust pie

Follow the recipe for Classic Pumpkin Pie (No. 219), adding 1
cup of coarsely chopped pecans to the hot filling. Bake as directed.

NO. 222   **PUMPKIN CHIFFON PIE**
                          One 9-inch single-crust pie

Prebaked 9-inch pie shell
(Gingersnap Crust)
  1 **envelope unflavored**   ¼ **teaspoon nutmeg**
    gelatin   ¼ **teaspoon allspice**
  ¼ **cup cold water**   1¼ **cups canned pumpkin**
  ¾ **cup dark brown sugar,**   **purée**
    firmly packed   3 **eggs, separated**
  2 **tablespoons dark molasses**   ½ **cup milk**
  ½ **teaspoon salt**   6 **tablespoons sugar**
  2 **teaspoons cinnamon**
  ½ **teaspoon ground ginger**

Prepare the prebaked pie shell; cool completely.
  Mix together the gelatin and water. Set aside. Combine the
brown sugar, molasses, salt, cinnamon, ginger, nutmeg, allspice,
and pumpkin. Mix well. Beat the egg yolks until light and foamy.
Add the milk to the egg yolks. Stir the egg yolk mixture into the
pumpkin mixture and turn into the top of a double boiler set over
simmering water. Cook, stirring frequently, for 10 minutes. Remove
the pan from the heat. Beat in the gelatin mixture. Chill until
slightly set. Beat the egg whites until they form stiff peaks. Gradually beat the sugar into the egg whites. Fold the egg white mixture
into the custard. Turn the filling into the pie shell. Chill until set.

NO. 223   **PUMPKIN MOLASSES PIE**

One 9-inch single-crust pie

**Pastry for a 9-inch single-crust pie
(Classic Single Crust)**

½ cup sugar	2 cups canned pumpkin
1 teaspoon cinnamon	purée
¾ teaspoon nutmeg	¼ cup dark molasses
¼ teaspoon ground ginger	2 cups heavy cream
¼ teaspoon salt	3 eggs, separated

Preheat the oven to 450° F. Prepare the pie pastry. Line the pie pan with the dough. Trim and crimp the edges.

Combine the sugar with the cinnamon, nutmeg, ginger, and salt. Mix in the pumpkin. Add the molasses and cream. Mix well. Beat the egg yolks and stir into the pumpkin mixture. Beat the egg whites until they form stiff peaks. Fold the egg whites into the pumpkin mixture. Turn the filling into the pie shell.

Bake at 450° F for 10 minutes. Reduce the heat to 325° F and bake 30 minutes more or until golden brown.

NO. 224   **PUMPKIN MINCE PIE**

One 9-inch single-crust pie

Follow the recipe for Pumpkin Molasses Pie (No. 223), adding ½ cup of ready-to-use mincemeat and 1 teaspoon of grated orange zest to the pumpkin mixture. Bake as directed.

NO. 225   **BLUE RIBBON PUMPKIN PIE**

One 9-inch single-crust pie

Follow the recipe for Pumpkin Molasses Pie (No. 223), adding 2 tablespoons of brandy, 1 tablespoon of crystallized ginger, 1 teaspoon of grated orange zest, and 2 tablespoons of orange juice to the pumpkin mixture. Bake as directed.

NO. 226   **PUMPKIN ORANGE PIE**

One 9-inch single-crust pie

Pastry for a 9-inch single-crust pie
(Classic Single Crust)

½ cup sugar	2 eggs, beaten
¼ teaspoon salt	1 cup canned pumpkin
½ teaspoon cinnamon	purée
¼ teaspoon nutmeg	½ cup heavy cream
⅛ teaspoon ground ginger	½ cup orange juice
⅛ teaspoon ground cloves	½ teaspoon grated orange
	zest

Preheat the oven to 450° F. Prepare the pie pastry. Line the pie pan with the dough. Trim and crimp the edges.

Mix together the sugar, salt, cinnamon, nutmeg, ginger, and cloves. Add the eggs, pumpkin, cream, orange juice, and orange zest. Stir well. Turn the filling into the crust.

Bake at 450° F for 10 minutes. Reduce the heat to 325° F and bake 50 minutes more or until golden brown.

NO. 227   **PUMPKIN ORANGE MERINGUE PIE**

One 9-inch single-crust pie

Recipe for Pumpkin Orange Pie (No. 226)

Meringue

3 large egg whites, at room	¼ teaspoon cream of tartar
temperature	6 tablespoons superfine
½ teaspoon vanilla extract	sugar

Prepare the recipe for Pumpkin Orange Pie. Bake as directed.

While the pie is still hot, prepare the meringue. Preheat the oven to 350° F. Beat the egg whites, vanilla, and cream of tartar until the mixture holds stiff peaks. Gradually add the sugar, 1 tablespoon at a time, beating until very stiff and glossy. All the sugar must be dissolved. Spread the meringue over the pie filling, sealing it to the edge of the crust. Bake 12 to 15 minutes or until golden brown. Cool before serving.

NO. 228   **RICH PUMPKIN PIE**

One 9-inch single-crust pie

Pastry for a 9-inch single-crust pie
(Classic Single Crust)

¾ cup sugar	½ teaspoon salt
1 teaspoon cinnamon	2 cups canned pumpkin
¾ teaspoon nutmeg	purée
⅜ teaspoon ground ginger	2 cups heavy cream
	3 eggs, separated

Preheat the oven to 450° F. Prepare the pie pastry. Line the pie pan with the dough. Trim and crimp the edges.

Mix together the sugar, cinnamon, nutmeg, ginger, and salt. Stir in the pumpkin and cream. Beat in the egg yolks. Beat the egg whites until they form stiff peaks. Fold in the egg whites. Turn the filling into the crust.

Bake at 450° F for 10 minutes. Reduce the heat to 325° F and bake 30 minutes more or until golden brown.

NO. 229   **CARROT PUMPKIN PIE**

One 9-inch single-crust pie

Follow the recipe for Rich Pumpkin Pie (No. 228), substituting 1 cup of steamed carrot purée for 1 cup of the pumpkin purée. Bake as directed.

NO. 230   **HONEY PUMPKIN PIE**

One 9-inch single-crust pie

Follow the recipe for Rich Pumpkin Pie (No. 228), substituting ½ cup of honey for the sugar. Bake as directed.

NO. 231   **VERY SPICY PUMPKIN PIE**
                                         One 9-inch single-crust pie

Pastry for a 9-inch single-crust pie
(Classic Single Crust)

1 cup dark brown sugar, firmly packed	⅛ teaspoon mace
½ teaspoon salt	¼ teaspoon allspice
¾ teaspoon cinnamon	⅛ teaspoon white pepper
¾ teaspoon nutmeg	2 cups canned pumpkin purée
⅜ teaspoon ground ginger	2 cups heavy cream
⅛ teaspoon ground cloves	3 eggs, separated

Preheat the oven to 450° F. Prepare the pie pastry. Line the pie pan with the dough. Trim and crimp the edges.

Mix together the sugar, salt, cinnamon, nutmeg, ginger, cloves, mace, allspice, and pepper. Add the pumpkin and cream. Mix well. Beat the egg yolks and add to the pumpkin mixture. Beat the egg whites until they form stiff peaks. Fold into the pumpkin mixture. Turn the filling into the crust.

Bake at 450° F for 10 minutes. Reduce the heat to 325° F and bake 30 minutes more or until golden brown.

NO. 232   **SQUASH PIE**
                                         One 9-inch single-crust pie

Pastry for a 9-inch single-crust pie
(Classic Single Crust)

2 cups cooked, strained squash	½ teaspoon salt
¾ cup dark brown sugar, firmly packed	½ teaspoon cinnamon
2 cups heavy cream	½ teaspoon nutmeg
3 eggs, beaten	½ teaspoon ground ginger

Preheat the oven to 450° F. Prepare the pie pastry. Line the pie pan with the dough. Trim and crimp the edges.

Mix together the squash, sugar, and cream. Add the eggs, salt, cinnamon, nutmeg, and ginger. Mix well. Turn the filling into the crust.

Bake at 450° F for 10 minutes. Reduce the heat to 325° F and bake 30 minutes more or until golden brown.

NO. 233   **SQUASH BEER PIE**

One 9-inch single-crust pie

Pastry for a 9-inch single-crust pie
(Classic Single Crust)

1½ cups cooked, strained
    squash
½ cup dark brown sugar,
    firmly packed
½ teaspoon salt
½ teaspoon ground cloves
½ teaspoon ground ginger

½ teaspoon cinnamon
2 tablespoons flour
1 cup cold beer
3 egg yolks, beaten

Meringue

3 large egg whites, at room
    temperature
½ teaspoon vanilla extract

¼ teaspoon cream of tartar
6 tablespoons superfine
    sugar

Preheat the oven to 350° F. Prepare the pie pastry. Line the pie pan with the dough. Trim and crimp the edges.

Combine the squash, sugar, salt, cloves, ginger, cinnamon, flour, beer, and egg yolks. Mix well. Turn the filling into the crust. Bake 1 hour.

While the pie is still hot, prepare the meringue. Beat the egg whites, vanilla, and cream of tartar until the mixture holds stiff peaks. Gradually add the sugar, 1 tablespoon at a time, beating until very stiff and glossy. All the sugar must be dissolved. Spread the meringue over the pie filling, sealing it to the edge of the crust. Bake at 350° F for 12 to 15 minutes or until golden brown. Cool before serving.

NO. 234   **SWEET POTATO PIE**
                          One 9-inch single-crust pie

Pastry for a 9-inch single-crust pie
(Classic Single Crust)

2 cups milk	½ teaspoon salt
2 tablespoons grated orange zest	½ teaspoon cinnamon
	½ teaspoon nutmeg
¼ cup orange juice	¼ cup unsalted butter or margarine
1½ cups cooked sweet potato purée	3 eggs, separated
½ cup dark brown sugar, firmly packed	

Preheat the oven to 425° F. Prepare the pie pastry. Line the pie pan with the dough. Trim and crimp the edges.

Scald the milk. Add the orange zest. Remove from heat and stir in the orange juice, sweet potato, sugar, salt, cinnamon, nutmeg, and butter. Beat the egg yolks and stir into the sweet potato mixture. Beat the egg whites until they form stiff peaks. Fold in the egg whites. Turn the filling into the crust.

Bake at 425° F for 10 minutes. Reduce the heat to 350° F and bake 35 minutes more or until golden brown.

NO. 235   **PECAN SWEET POTATO PIE**
                          One 9-inch single-crust pie

Follow the recipe for Sweet Potato Pie (No. 234), adding ¾ of a cup of coarsely chopped pecans to the sweet potato mixture. Bake as directed.

NO. 236   **SWEET POTATO MERINGUE PIE**
                          One 9-inch single-crust pie

Recipe for Sweet Potato Pie (No. 234)

Meringue

3 large egg whites, at room temperature	¼ teaspoon cream of tartar
½ teaspoon vanilla extract	6 tablespoons superfine sugar

Prepare the recipe for Sweet Potato Pie. Bake as directed.

While the pie is still hot, prepare the meringue. Preheat the oven to 350° F. Beat the egg whites, vanilla, and cream of tartar until the mixture holds stiff peaks. Gradually add the sugar, 1 tablespoon at a time, beating until very stiff and glossy. All the sugar must be dissolved. Spread the meringue over the pie filling, sealing it to the edge of the crust. Bake 12 to 15 minutes or until golden brown. Cool before serving.

NO. 237

WHITE POTATO PIE

One 9-inch single-crust pie

Pastry for a 9-inch single-crust pie (Classic Single Crust)

1½ cups hot mashed potatoes	2 eggs, separated
2 tablespoons unsalted butter or margarine	2 cups milk
	2 tablespoons lemon juice
½ cup sugar	1 tablespoon grated lemon
¼ teaspoon salt	zest

Preheat the oven to 450° F. Prepare the pie pastry. Line the pie pan with the dough. Trim and crimp the edges.

Mix together the mashed potatoes, butter, sugar, and salt. Cool to room temperature. Beat the egg yolks. Combine the potato mixture with the egg yolks, milk, lemon juice, and lemon zest. Mix well. Beat the egg whites until they form stiff peaks. Fold the egg whites into the potato mixture. Turn the filling into the crust.

Bake at 450° F for 10 minutes. Reduce the heat to 325° F and bake 30 minutes more or until golden brown.

Ice Cream and Other Frozen Pies

With an extra pan in the cupboard and a little advance planning, a scrumptious ice cream pie can always be ready in the freezer for unexpected guests or a gala summer dessert. These simple yet amply rewarding frozen pies never see an oven except for an 8-minute prebaked crust or the occasional meringue. An ice cream maker opens infinite possibilities for creating additional frozen pies and other icy confections.

NO. 238   **CHERRY ICE CREAM PIE**

One 9-inch single-crust pie

Prebaked 9-inch pie shell
(Graham Cracker Crust)

  1 envelope unflavored
     gelatin
  2 tablespoons sugar
  1 cup cherry juice

  1 tablespoon lemon juice
  1 pint vanilla ice cream
  3 cups halved, pitted fresh
     sweet cherries

Prepare the prebaked pie shell; cool completely.

Mix together the gelatin and sugar. Set aside. Combine the cherry and lemon juices and bring to a boil. Add the gelatin mixture and stir until dissolved. Remove the pan from the heat. Stir in the ice cream. Mix well. Add the cherries. Chill until slightly thickened. Turn the filling into the pie shell. Freeze until set.

NO. 239   **CHERRY BLUEBERRY ICE CREAM PIE**

One 9-inch single-crust pie

Follow the recipe for Cherry Ice Cream Pie (No. 238), substituting 1½ cups of fresh blueberries for 1½ cups of cherries.

NO. 240   **BLUEBERRY GRAPE ICE CREAM PIE**

One 9-inch single-crust pie

Prebaked 9-inch pie shell
(Graham Cracker Crust)

  1 envelope unflavored
     gelatin
  2 tablespoons sugar
  1 cup grape juice

  1 tablespoon lemon juice
  1 pint vanilla ice cream
  3 cups fresh blueberries

Prepare the prebaked pie shell; cool completely.

Mix together the gelatin and sugar. Set aside. Combine the grape and lemon juices and bring to a boil. Add the gelatin mixture and stir until dissolved. Remove the pan from the heat. Stir in the ice cream. Mix well. Chill until slightly thickened. Add the blueberries. Turn the filling into the pie shell. Freeze until set.

NO. 241   **STRAWBERRY ICE CREAM PIE**
                                        One 9-inch single-crust pie

Follow the recipe for Blueberry Grape Ice Cream Pie (No. 240),
substituting strawberry juice for grape juice and fresh, sliced strawberries for blueberries.

NO. 242   **PEACH ICE CREAM PIE**
                                        One 9-inch single-crust pie

Follow the recipe for Blueberry Grape Ice Cream Pie (No. 240),
substituting peach nectar for grape juice and peeled, sliced peaches
for blueberries.

NO. 243   **CHOCOLATE FUDGE ICE CREAM**
                                                                    PIE
                                        One 9-inch single-crust pie

Prebaked 9-inch pie shell
(Chocolate Crust)

- 3 ounces (3 squares) unsweetened baking chocolate
- ⅔ cup sugar
- ¼ cup heavy cream
- 1 tablespoon unsalted butter or margarine
- 1 teaspoon vanilla extract
- 1 pint chocolate ice cream, softened
- ½ cup walnuts, coarsely chopped

Meringue

- 3 large egg whites, at room temperature
- ½ teaspoon vanilla extract
- ¼ teaspoon cream of tartar
- 6 tablespoons superfine sugar

Prepare the prebaked pie shell; cool completely.

In a saucepan, combine the chocolate, sugar, and cream. Bring
to a boil and cook, stirring constantly, until the mixture reaches
the soft-ball stage (when a teaspoon of the mixture dropped into
a glass of water forms a soft ball). Remove the pan from the heat.
Stir in the butter and vanilla. Cool to room temperature.

Pour half the fudge filling into the pie shell. Top with half the ice cream. Sprinkle on half the walnuts. Layer on the remaining fudge, ice cream, and walnuts. Freeze at least 12 hours.

When the pie is frozen solid, prepare the meringue. Preheat the oven to 475° F. Beat the egg whites, vanilla, and cream of tartar until the mixture holds stiff peaks. Gradually add the sugar, 1 tablespoon at a time, beating until very stiff and glossy. All the sugar must be dissolved. Spread the meringue over the pie, sealing it to the edge of the crust. Bake 5 to 6 minutes or until golden brown. Serve immediately.

NO. 244   **COFFEE FUDGE ICE CREAM PIE**
One 9-inch single-crust pie

Follow the recipe for Chocolate Fudge Ice Cream Pie (No. 243), adding 2 tablespoons of freshly brewed coffee to the fudge mixture and substituting coffee ice cream for chocolate ice cream.

NO. 245   **PEPPERMINT FUDGE ICE CREAM PIE**
One 9-inch single-crust pie

Follow the recipe for Chocolate Fudge Ice Cream Pie (No. 243), substituting crushed peppermint candy for the walnuts and peppermint ice cream for chocolate ice cream.

NO. 246   **LEMON LIME ICE CREAM PIE**
One 9-inch single-crust pie

Prebaked 9-inch pie shell
(Graham Cracker Crust)

2 envelopes unflavored gelatin	1¼ cups water
¾ cup sugar	1 teaspoon grated lemon zest
¼ cup lemon juice	1 teaspoon grated lime zest
½ cup lime juice	1 pint vanilla ice cream

Prepare the prebaked pie shell; cool completely.

Mix together the gelatin and sugar. Set aside. Combine the lemon juice, lime juice, and water and bring to a boil. Add the gelatin mixture and stir until dissolved. Remove the pan from the heat. Add the lemon and lime zests. Stir in the ice cream. Mix well. Chill until slightly thickened. Turn the filling into the pie shell. Freeze until set.

NO. 247   **STRAWBERRY CHEESE PIE**

One 9-inch single-crust pie

Prebaked 9-inch pie shell
(Graham Cracker Crust)

16 ounces cream cheese, at room temperature	2 eggs, beaten
⅔ cup sugar	1 teaspoon vanilla extract

Topping

1 cup sour cream	1 cup sliced fresh
2 tablespoons sugar	strawberries or
½ teaspoon vanilla extract	strawberry sauce

Prepare the prebaked pie shell; cool completely.

Preheat the oven to 375° F. Beat the cream cheese until smooth. Add the sugar. Beat in the eggs, one at a time. Add the vanilla. Turn the filling into the pie shell.

Bake 20 minutes. Remove the pie from the oven and increase the oven temperature to 500° F.

Prepare the topping. Beat the sour cream with the sugar and vanilla. Pour the topping over the pie. Bake 5 minutes. Cool, then freeze until set. Serve with strawberries or strawberry sauce.

NO. 248   **RASPBERRY CHEESE PIE**

One 9-inch single-crust pie

Follow the recipe for Strawberry Cheese Pie (No. 247), substituting raspberries for strawberries. Bake as directed for strawberry cheese pie.

NO. 249   **STRAWBERRY YOGURT PIE**

One 9-inch single-crust pie

Prebaked 9-inch pie shell
(Graham Cracker Crust)

1 cup heavy cream	1 cup plain yogurt
⅓ cup sugar	2 cups strawberry yogurt
1 teaspoon vanilla extract	1 cup sliced fresh strawberries

Prepare the prebaked pie shell; cool completely.

Whip the cream until stiff. Gradually beat in the sugar. Add the vanilla. Combine the whipped cream with the yogurt. Mix well. Add the strawberries. Turn the filling into the pie shell. Freeze until set.

NO. 250   ## RASPBERRY YOGURT PIE
One 9-inch single-crust pie

Follow the recipe for Strawberry Yogurt Pie (No. 249), substituting raspberry yogurt for strawberry yogurt and raspberries for strawberries.

NO. 251   ## BLUEBERRY YOGURT PIE
One 9-inch single-crust pie

Follow the recipe for Strawberry Yogurt Pie (No. 249), substituting blueberry yogurt for strawberry yogurt and blueberries for strawberries.

NO. 252   ## PEACH YOGURT PIE
One 9-inch single-crust pie

Follow the recipe for Strawberry Yogurt Pie (No. 249), substituting peach yogurt for strawberry yogurt and peeled, sliced peaches for strawberries.

NO. 253   ## MIXED FRUIT YOGURT PIE
One 9-inch single-crust pie

Follow the recipe for Strawberry Yogurt Pie (No. 249), substituting 3 cups of prepared mixed fresh fruit for the strawberries.

Special Pies

When is a pie not a pie? When it's a Boston cream pie! Even under the broad definition of pie as anything baked in a crust, some recipes are just too special for a specific pie category. The delicious exceptions in this chapter include Boston cream pie, angel pie with a distinctive meringue crust, fudge pie, Kentucky pie with whiskey and chocolate morsels, marmalade pie, sugar pie, shoo fly pie, and a cornucopia of pecan pies for all tastes.

ANGEL PIE

One 9-inch single-crust pie

Prebaked 9-inch pie shell
(Meringue Crust)

- 4 egg yolks
- 2 cups sugar
- 2 tablespoons flour
- ¼ cup lemon juice

- ¼ cup boiling water
- ½ teaspoon almond extract
- 1 cup heavy cream

Prepare the prebaked pie shell; cool completely.

Beat the egg yolks until light and foamy. Gradually beat in the sugar. Add the flour. Turn the mixture into the top of a double boiler set over simmering water. Slowly stir in the lemon juice and boiling water. Cook, stirring constantly, until thickened. Remove the pan from the heat. Stir in the almond extract. Chill until slightly thickened. Turn the filling into the pie shell. Whip the cream and spread on top of the filling. Chill for 6 to 7 hours.

BOSTON CREAM PIE

One 8-inch layer cake

- 1¾ cups sifted cake flour
- 1 cup sugar
- ¼ teaspoon salt
- 2½ teaspoons baking powder

- ⅓ cup unsalted butter or margarine, softened
- ⅔ cup milk
- 1 egg
- 1 teaspoon vanilla extract

Filling

- ½ cup sugar
- 5 tablespoons flour
- 1 egg, beaten

- 1½ cups milk
- 1 teaspoon vanilla extract

Icing

- 1 ounce (1 square) unsweetened baking chocolate
- 1 tablespoon unsalted butter or margarine

- 3½ tablespoons boiling water
- 1 cup confectioners' sugar

Preheat the oven to 350° F. Thoroughly butter the bottom and sides of two 8-inch springform or layer cake pans. Sift together the flour, sugar, salt, and baking powder. Add the butter, milk, egg, and vanilla all at once. Beat for 2 minutes. Pour half of the batter into each pan.

Bake 25 to 35 minutes or until a toothpick inserted in the cakes comes out clean.

While the cakes are cooling, prepare the filling. In the top of a double boiler set over simmering water, combine the sugar and flour. Beat the egg with the milk and slowly stir into the sugar mixture. Cook, stirring frequently, about 20 minutes or until thickened. Remove the pan from the heat. Stir in the vanilla and cool to room temperature. Remove the cakes from the pans and place on a serving plate. Spread the custard over one of the cakes and place the remaining cake on top.

To prepare the icing, melt the chocolate and butter together over very low heat. Remove the pan from the heat. Stir in the boiling water and sugar. Beat until smooth. Ice the top of the cake and let the icing set. Serve in wedge-shaped "pie" slices.

NO. 256   **COFFEE TOFFEE PIE**

One 9-inch single-crust pie

Prebaked 9-inch pie shell
(Chocolate Crust or Walnut Crust)

½ cup unsalted butter or
   margarine, softened
¾ cup sugar
1 ounce (1 square)
   unsweetened chocolate,
   melted and cooled

2 teaspoons instant coffee
   powder
2 eggs

Topping

2 cups heavy cream
2 tablespoons instant coffee
   powder

½ cup confectioners' sugar
Chocolate shavings

Prepare the prebaked pie shell; cool completely.

Cream together the butter and sugar. Beat in the chocolate and coffee powder. Beat in the eggs, one at a time. Turn the filling into the pie shell. Refrigerate overnight.

The next day, prepare the topping. Combine the cream, coffee powder, and sugar. Cover and chill for 1 hour. Beat the cream mixture until stiff. Layer the topping over the filling and decorate with chocolate shavings. Chill for 2 hours before serving.

NO. 257 CHOCOLATE TOFFEE PIE
One 9-inch single-crust pie

Follow the recipe for Coffee Toffee Pie (No. 256), substituting
unsweetened cocoa power for instant coffee powder.

NO. 258 CHEESECAKE PIE
One 9-inch single-crust pie

Pastry for a 9-inch single-crust pie
(Vanilla Wafer Crust)

16 ounces cream cheese, at room temperature	1 teaspoon vanilla extract
1 cup sugar	4 eggs, separated
2 tablespoons flour	1 cup heavy cream
¼ teaspoon salt	

Preheat the oven to 325° F. Prepare the pie pastry. Line the pie
pan with the dough. Trim and crimp the edges.

Beat the cream cheese until smooth. Mix together the sugar,
flour, and salt. Add the sugar mixture to the cream cheese. Beat
in the vanilla and egg yolks. Stir in the cream. Beat the egg whites
until they form stiff peaks. Fold in the egg whites. Turn the filling
into the crust.

Bake 1 hour.

NO. 259 FUDGE PIE
One 9-inch single-crust pie

Prebaked 9-inch pie shell
(Classic Single Crust or Walnut Crust)

1 cup semi-sweet chocolate morsels	1¼ cups sweetened condensed milk
1½ cups crushed vanilla wafers	1 teaspoon vanilla extract
½ cup walnuts, coarsely chopped	Sweetened whipped cream

Prepare the prebaked pie shell; cool completely.

Preheat the oven to 375° F. In the top of a double boiler set
over simmering water, melt the chocolate. Mix together the vanilla

wafers and walnuts. Stir in the milk, the vanilla, and chocolate. Mix well. Turn the filling into the pie shell.

Bake 30 minutes. Serve with sweetened whipped cream.

NO. 260   **KENTUCKY PIE**

One 9-inch single-crust pie

Prebaked 9-inch pie shell
(Classic Single Crust)

2 eggs	3 tablespoons whiskey
1 cup sugar	1 cup walnuts, coarsely
½ cup flour	chopped
½ cup unsalted butter or	1 cup semi-sweet chocolate
margarine, melted and	morsels
cooled	

Prepare the prebaked pie shell; cool completely.

Preheat the oven to 350° F. Beat the eggs until light and foamy. Gradually beat in the sugar. Mix in the flour, butter, whiskey, walnuts, and chocolate morsels. Turn the filling into the pie shell.

Bake 35 minutes.

NO. 261   **MACAROON PIE**

One 9-inch single-crust pie

Prebaked 9-inch pie shell
(Classic Single Crust)

3 tablespoons flour	½ teaspoon almond extract
½ cup sugar	12 macaroons, crumbled
3 egg yolks, beaten	Toasted almonds
2 cups milk	

Prepare the prebaked pie shell; cool completely.

In the top of a double boiler set over simmering water, combine the flour and sugar. In a separate bowl, combine the egg yolks and milk. Slowly stir the egg yolk mixture into the sugar mixture. Cook, stirring frequently, about 20 minutes or until thickened. Remove the pan from the heat. Stir in the almond extract and macaroons. Cool until slightly thickened. Turn the filling into the pie shell. Sprinkle with almonds. Chill until set.

NO. 262   **MAPLE RAISIN WALNUT PIE**

One 9-inch single-crust pie

Pastry for a 9-inch single-crust pie
(Classic Single Crust)

1 cup raisins	2 eggs, beaten
3 tablespoons flour	1½ cups walnuts, coarsely
¼ cup unsalted butter or	chopped
margarine, softened	1 cup maple syrup
½ cup shaved maple sugar	⅛ teaspoon nutmeg

Preheat the oven to 450° F. Prepare the pie pastry. Line the pie pan with the dough. Trim and crimp the edges.

Mix together the raisins and 1 tablespoon of the flour. Arrange the raisin mixture in the bottom of the pie shell. Cream the butter. Beat in the maple sugar, eggs, and remaining flour. Mix well. Stir in the walnuts, maple syrup, and nutmeg. Turn the filling into the crust.

Bake at 450° F for 10 minutes. Reduce the heat to 325° F and bake 30 to 35 minutes more or until golden brown.

NO. 263   **MOLASSES PIE**

One 9-inch single-crust pie

Pastry for a 9-inch single-crust pie
(Classic Single Crust)

2 eggs	1 tablespoon unsalted butter
1 cup sugar	or margarine
½ cup dark molasses	2 tablespoons bread crumbs
½ teaspoon nutmeg	¾ cup milk
	¼ cup cider vinegar

Preheat the oven to 450° F. Prepare the pie pastry. Line the pie pan with the dough. Trim and crimp the edges.

Beat the eggs until light and foamy. Beat in the sugar and molasses. Add the nutmeg, butter, bread crumbs, milk, and vinegar. Mix well. Turn the filling into the crust.

Bake at 450° F for 10 minutes. Reduce the heat to 350° F and bake 30 minutes more.

NO. 264   **MINCE PIE**
One 9-inch double-crust pie

Pastry for a 9-inch double-
    crust pie
(Classic Double Crust)
  4 cups peeled, cored,   2 tablespoons unsalted
      coarsely chopped apples   butter or margarine
  1 cup dark raisins   1 tablespoon cider vinegar
  1 cup golden raisins   2 teaspoons cinnamon
  ¼ cup candied orange peel   1 teaspoon allspice
  ¼ cup candied lemon peel   ¼ teaspoon nutmeg
  1 teaspoon grated lemon   ¼ teaspoon black pepper
      zest   1½ cups water
1¼ cups dark brown sugar,   ½ cup rum
      firmly packed   Vanilla ice cream

One day before baking the pie, prepare the mincemeat. In a large
saucepan, combine the apples, raisins, orange and lemon peels,
lemon zest, sugar, butter, vinegar, cinnamon, allspice, nutmeg,
pepper, and water. Mix well and bring to a boil. Reduce the heat
to low and simmer, stirring frequently, for 40 minutes. Add the
rum and continue to cook for 10 minutes, or until the mixture is
almost dry. Cool to room temperature. Cover, and chill overnight.

The next day, preheat the oven to 425° F. Prepare the pie pastry.
Line the pie pan with the bottom crust, using half the dough.
Keep the remaining dough chilled.

Turn the prepared mince filling into the pie shell. Roll out the
top crust and lay it on the filling. Trim off any excess dough, crimp
the edges, and prick with the tines of a fork to vent.

Bake at 425° F for 30 minutes. Reduce the heat to 375° F and
bake 25 minutes more or until golden brown. Serve with vanilla
ice cream.

NO. 265   **ORANGE MARMALADE PIE**

One 9-inch lattice-top pie

Pastry for a 9-inch lattice-top pie
(Lemon Crust)

2 cups orange marmalade	1 tablespoon cold water
2 tablespoons brandy	1 tablespoon sugar
1 egg yolk	

Preheat the oven to 400° F. Prepare the pie pastry. Line the pie pan with the bottom crust, using half of the dough. Keep the remaining dough chilled. Prick the bottom of the pie with the tines of a fork. Line the shell with waxed paper or baking parchment, and fill with baking weights such as dried beans or aluminum pellets.

Bake 10 minutes. Remove the pie from the oven and remove the beans and waxed paper. Leave the oven on.

In a saucepan, combine the marmalade and brandy. Cook over low heat, stirring constantly, until liquid. Pour the marmalade mixture into the pie shell. Roll out, cut, and lay on the lattice strips. Mix together the egg yolk and water. Brush the glaze over the lattice strips and sprinkle with sugar.

Return the pie to the oven and bake 15 to 20 minutes more or until golden brown.

NO. 266   **ORANGE MARMALADE HAZELNUT PIE**

One 9-inch lattice-top pie

Follow the recipe for Orange Marmalade Pie (No. 265), adding ½ cup of finely chopped hazelnuts to the filling. Bake as directed.

NO. 267   **OATMEAL WALNUT PIE**

One 9-inch single-crust pie

Pastry for a 9-inch single-crust pie
(Classic Single Crust)

2 eggs, beaten
¾ cup dark molasses
½ cup light brown sugar,
  firmly packed
½ cup heavy cream
¾ cup rolled oats

1 tablespoon unsalted butter
  or margarine, melted
1 teaspoon cinnamon
½ cup walnuts, coarsely
  chopped
Sweetened whipped cream

Preheat the oven to 350° F. Prepare the pie pastry. Line the pie
pan with the dough. Trim and crimp the edges.

Mix together the eggs, molasses, sugar, cream, oats, butter,
cinnamon, and walnuts. Turn the filling into the crust.

Bake 40 to 45 minutes or until a knife inserted in the center
of the pie comes out clean. Serve warm, with sweetened whipped
cream.

NO. 268   **PEANUT PIE**

One 9-inch single-crust pie

Pastry for a 9-inch single-crust pie
(Classic Single Crust)

¾ cup dark corn syrup
½ cup light brown sugar,
  firmly packed
⅓ cup unsalted butter or
  margarine, melted
3 eggs, beaten

¼ cup bourbon
1 teaspoon grated lemon
  zest
1½ cups unsalted roasted
  peanuts, coarsely
  chopped

Preheat the oven to 350° F. Prepare the pie pastry. Line the pie
pan with the dough. Trim and crimp the edges.

Mix together the corn syrup, sugar, butter, eggs, bourbon, lemon
zest, and ¾ cup of the peanuts. Turn the filling into the crust.
Sprinkle the remaining peanuts on top of the filling.

Bake 50 minutes or until a knife inserted in the center of the
pie comes out clean.

NO. 269   **PEANUT BUTTER PIE**

One 9-inch single-crust pie

Pastry for a 9-inch single-crust pie
(Classic Single Crust)

1 cup dark corn syrup	1 teaspoon vanilla extract
1 cup sugar	⅓ cup peanut butter
3 eggs, beaten	

Preheat the oven to 450° F. Prepare the pie pastry. Line the pie pan with the dough. Trim and crimp the edges.

Combine the corn syrup, sugar, eggs, vanilla, and peanut butter. Mix well. Turn the filling into the crust.

Bake at 450° F for 10 minutes. Reduce the heat to 325° F and bake 45 minutes more or until a knife inserted in the center of the pie comes out clean.

NO. 270   **PECAN PIE I**

One 9-inch single-crust pie

Pastry for a 9-inch single-crust pie
(Classic Single Crust)

¼ cup unsalted butter or margarine, softened	1 teaspoon vanilla extract
½ cup dark brown sugar, firmly packed	1 cup pecans, coarsely chopped
1 cup light corn syrup	Sweetened whipped cream
3 eggs, beaten	

Preheat the oven to 450° F. Prepare the pie pastry. Line the pie pan with the dough. Trim and crimp the edges.

Cream together the butter and sugar. Beat in the corn syrup, eggs, and vanilla. Stir in the pecans. Turn the filling into the crust.

Bake at 450° F for 10 minutes. Reduce the heat to 325° F and bake 30 minutes more. Serve with sweetened whipped cream.

NO. 271   **WALNUT PIE I**

One 9-inch single-crust pie

Follow the recipe for Pecan Pie I (No. 270), substituting walnuts for pecans. Bake as directed.

PECAN PIE II
                                        One 9-inch single-crust pie

Pastry for a 9-inch single-crust pie
(Classic Single Crust)

3 eggs, beaten	1 cup sugar
1 cup dark corn syrup	1 cup whole pecans
1 teaspoon vanilla extract	Sweetened whipped cream

Preheat the oven to 450° F. Prepare the pie pastry. Line the pie pan with the dough. Trim and crimp the edges.

Combine the eggs, corn syrup, vanilla, and sugar. Mix well. Stir in the pecans. Turn the filling into the crust.

Bake at 450° F for 10 minutes. Reduce the heat to 350° F and bake 30 minutes more. Serve with sweetened whipped cream.

WALNUT PIE II
                                        One 9-inch single-crust pie

Follow the recipe for Pecan Pie II (No. 272), substituting walnuts for pecans. Bake as directed.

SOUR CREAM PECAN PIE
                                        One 9-inch single-crust pie

Pastry for a 9-inch single-crust pie
(Classic Single Crust)

½ cup dark brown sugar, firmly packed	¾ cup sour cream
	1 teaspoon vanilla extract
⅓ cup unsalted butter or margarine	1 teaspoon grated orange zest
4 eggs	1 cup pecans, coarsely chopped
½ cup sugar	
½ cup light corn syrup	

Preheat the oven to 350° F. Prepare the pie pastry. Line the pie pan with the dough. Trim and crimp the edges.

In the top of a double boiler set over simmering water, combine the brown sugar and butter. Cook, stirring frequently, until the butter is melted. Remove the pan from the heat.

Beat the eggs until light and foamy. Gradually beat in the sugar.

Add the corn syrup and sour cream. Slowly pour the egg mixture into the butter mixture. Return to the double boiler and cook, stirring constantly, for 5 minutes. Remove the pan from the heat. Stir in the vanilla, orange zest, and pecans. Turn the filling into the crust.

Bake 40 minutes.

NO. 275   ## SOUR CREAM WALNUT PIE

One 9-inch single-crust pie

Follow the recipe for Sour Cream Pecan Pie (No. 274), substituting walnuts for pecans. Bake as directed.

NO. 276   ## PIEBALD PIE

One 9-inch single-crust pie

Prebaked 9-inch pie shell
(Chocolate Crust)
- ⅓ cup flour
- 1½ cups sugar
- 1½ cups boiling water
- 3 egg whites

- 1 cup packaged unsweetened shredded coconut
- ½ teaspoon almond extract
- ¼ cup chocolate shavings

Prepare the prebaked pie shell; cool completely.

In the top of a double boiler set over simmering water, combine the flour and sugar. Slowly add the boiling water, stirring constantly. Cook, stirring frequently, until thick and smooth, about 15 minutes. Cool slightly. Beat the egg whites until they form stiff peaks. Fold the egg whites into the mixture. Stir in the coconut and almond extract. Turn the filling into the pie shell. Sprinkle the chocolate shavings on top of the pie. Chill until set.

NO. 277   **LEMON WALNUT RICOTTA PIE**
                                    One 9-inch single-crust pie

Pastry for a 9-inch single-crust pie
(Classic Single Crust)

  2 cups ricotta cheese,   1 teaspoon grated lemon
     drained   zest
  ½ cup confectioners' sugar   ½ teaspoon lemon extract
  1 egg yolk, beaten   ½ cup walnuts, coarsely
                             chopped

Preheat the oven to 450° F. Prepare the pie pastry. Line the pie
pan with the dough. Trim and crimp the edges.

Mix together the ricotta, sugar, egg yolk, lemon zest, lemon
extract, and walnuts. Turn the filling into the crust.

Place the pie in the oven. Immediately reduce the heat to
400° F and bake for 30 minutes. Serve warm.

NO. 278   **CHOCOLATE CHIP RICOTTA PIE**
                                    One 9-inch single-crust pie

Follow the recipe for Lemon Walnut Ricotta Pie (No. 277), substituting vanilla extract for lemon extract and adding ½ cup of
semi-sweet chocolate morsels to the filling along with the walnuts.
Bake as directed.

NO. 279   **BUTTERSCOTCH CHIP RICOTTA**
                                                PIE
                                    One 9-inch single-crust pie

Follow the recipe for Lemon Walnut Ricotta Pie (No. 277), substituting vanilla extract for lemon extract and adding ½ cup of
butterscotch morsels to the filling along with the walnuts. Bake as
directed.

NO. 280   **SHOO FLY PIE**

A 9-inch crumb crust pie

Pastry for a 9-inch single-crust pie
(Classic Single Crust)

⅓ cup light brown sugar,   1 cup dark molasses
    firmly packed   1 teaspoon baking soda
¾ cup flour   1 cup boiling water
6 tablespoons unsalted
    butter or margarine
1 egg, beaten

Preheat the oven to 425° F. Prepare the pie pastry. Line the pie pan with the dough. Trim and crimp the edges.

Mix together the brown sugar and flour. Using a pastry blender or the tines of a fork, cut in the butter until the mixture is crumbly. Divide the crumbs in half.

Add the egg and molasses to one half of the crumbs. Mix well. Dissolve the baking soda in one quarter cup of the water. Add the baking soda mixture and the remaining water to the egg mixture. Turn the filling into the crust. Top with the remaining crumbs.

Bake at 425° F for 15 minutes. Reduce the heat to 350° F and bake 40 to 45 minutes more or until a knife inserted in the center of the pie comes out clean.

NO. 281   **STRAWBERRY JAM PIE**

One 9-inch single-crust pie

Pastry for a 9-inch single-crust pie
(Classic Single Crust)

3 egg yolks   1 cup strawberry jam
1 cup sour cream   ¼ cup sugar
2 tablespoons unsalted   1 tablespoon cornstarch
    butter or margarine,
    melted

Meringue

3 large egg whites, at room   ¼ teaspoon cream of tartar
    temperature   6 tablespoons superfine
½ teaspoon vanilla extract   sugar

Preheat the oven to 425° F. Prepare the pie pastry. Line the pie pan with the dough. Trim and crimp the edges.

Beat the egg yolks until light and foamy. Stir in the sour cream, butter, and jam. Mix together the sugar and cornstarch. Add the sugar mixture to the egg yolk mixture. Turn the filling into the crust.

Bake about 25 minutes. Remove the pie from the oven and reduce the oven temperature to 350° F.

While the pie is still hot, prepare the meringue. Beat the egg whites, vanilla, and cream of tartar until the mixture holds stiff peaks. Gradually add the sugar, 1 tablespoon at a time, beating until very stiff and glossy. All the sugar must be dissolved. Spread the meringue over the pie filling, sealing it to the edge of the crust. Bake 12 to 15 minutes or until golden brown. Cool before serving.

NO. 282   **SUGAR PIE**

One 9-inch single-crust pie

**Pastry for a 9-inch single-crust pie
(Classic Single Crust)**

3 eggs	1 teaspoon vanilla extract
3 cups light brown sugar, firmly packed	1 teaspoon grated lemon zest
½ cup milk	½ cup unsalted butter or margarine, melted

Preheat the oven to 450° F. Prepare the pie pastry. Line the pie pan with the dough. Trim and crimp the edges.

Beat the eggs until light and foamy. Gradually beat in the sugar. Add the milk, vanilla, lemon zest, and butter. Mix well. Turn the filling into the crust.

Bake at 450° F for 10 minutes. Reduce the heat to 325° F and bake 25 minutes more or until a knife inserted in the center of the pie comes out clean.

NO. 283   VANILLA CRUMB PIE

One 9-inch single-crust pie

Pastry for a 9-inch single-crust pie
(Classic Single Crust)

½ cup light brown sugar,   2 tablespoons flour
   firmly packed   1 teaspoon vanilla extract
½ cup dark molasses   1 teaspoon grated lemon
1 cup water   zest
1 egg, beaten

Topping

⅓ cup light brown sugar,   ½ teaspoon baking soda
   firmly packed   6 tablespoons unsalted
¾ cup flour   butter or margarine
½ teaspoon cinnamon

Preheat the oven to 375° F. Prepare the pie pastry. Line the pie pan with the dough. Trim and crimp the edges.

In the top of a double boiler set over simmering water, combine the sugar, molasses, water, egg, and flour. Mix well. Cook, stirring frequently, until thickened. Remove the pan from the heat. Stir in the vanilla and lemon zest. Cool slightly, then turn into the crust. To prepare the topping, mix together the sugar, flour, cinnamon, and baking soda. Using a pastry blender or the tines of a fork, cut in the butter until the mixture is crumbly. Sprinkle the crumbs evenly over the filled pie shell.

Bake 50 to 60 minutes or until golden brown.

NO. 284   CHOCOLATE CRUMB PIE

One 9-inch single-crust pie

Follow the recipe for Vanilla Crumb Pie (No. 283), adding ½ cup of semi-sweet chocolate morsels to the filling. Bake as directed for Vanilla Crumb Pie.

Quick-And-Easy Pies

There's always time for a quick-and-easy pie. With a commercial pudding mix, dessert miracles can be accomplished with little effort and to great effect. Purists may turn up their noses, but a quick and easy lemon meringue pie really looks like the real thing. Other tasty, time-saving recipes include chocolate almond mousse pie, coconut cream meringue pie, and strawberry shortcake pie. Unless otherwise specified, these pies use regular, *not* instant, pudding mixes.

NO. 285   **EASY BLACK FOREST PIE**

One 9-inch single-crust pie

**Prebaked 9-inch pie shell
(Chocolate Crust)**

1 package (3½ ounces)
    chocolate pudding mix
2 cups milk
1 cup sweetened whipped
    cream

1½ cups halved, pitted fresh
    sweet cherries
Chocolate shavings

Prepare the prebaked pie shell; cool completely.

Combine the pudding mix and milk in a saucepan. Bring the mixture to a full boil, stirring constantly. Remove the pan from the heat. Cool for 5 minutes. Fold in the whipped cream and cherries. Turn the filling into the pie shell. Sprinkle with chocolate shavings. Chill until set, at least 2 hours.

NO. 286   **EASY BUTTERSCOTCH PIE**

One 9-inch single-crust pie

**Prebaked 9-inch pie shell
(Graham Cracker Crust)**

1 package (3½ ounces)
    butterscotch pudding
    mix
2 cups milk

1 cup sweetened whipped
    cream
Chocolate shavings

Prepare the prebaked pie shell; cool completely.

Combine the pudding mix and milk in a saucepan. Bring the mixture to a full boil, stirring constantly. Remove the pan from the heat. Cool for 5 minutes. Fold in the whipped cream. Turn the filling into the pie shell. Sprinkle with chocolate shavings. Chill until set, at least 2 hours.

NO. 287   **EASY BUTTERSCOTCH CHOCOLATE
CHIP PIE**

One 9-inch single-crust pie

Follow the recipe for Easy Butterscotch Pie (No. 286), adding ½ cup of semi-sweet chocolate morsels to the cooled filling.

NO. **288**   **EASY VANILLA CHOCOLATE CHIP PIE**

One 9-inch single-crust pie

Follow the recipe for Easy Butterscotch Pie (No. 286), substituting vanilla pudding mix for butterscotch pudding mix and adding ½ cup of semi-sweet chocolate morsels to the cooled filling.

NO. **289**   **EASY CHOCOLATE ALMOND MOUSSE PIE**

One 9-inch single-crust pie

Prebaked 9-inch pie shell
(Graham Cracker Crust)
  1 package (3½ ounces)
     instant chocolate mousse
     mix
  1 cup milk

½ cup sour cream
¼ cup toasted slivered
    almonds

Prepare the prebaked pie shell; cool completely.

Beat the mousse mix with the milk until thick, about 3 minutes. Stir in the sour cream. Turn the filling into the pie shell. Sprinkle with toasted almonds. Chill until set, at least 2 hours.

NO. 290

EASY COCONUT CREAM MERINGUE PIE

One 9-inch single-crust pie

Prebaked 9-inch pie shell
(Classic Single Crust)
1 package (3½ ounces)
   coconut pudding mix
2 cups milk

1 cup packaged unsweetened
   shredded coconut

Meringue

3 large egg whites, at room
   temperature
½ teaspoon vanilla extract

¼ teaspoon cream of tartar
6 tablespoons superfine
   sugar

Prepare the prebaked pie shell; cool completely. Preheat the oven to 350° F.

Combine the pudding mix and milk in a saucepan. Bring the mixture to a full boil, stirring constantly. Remove the pan from the heat. Cool for 5 minutes. Mix in the coconut. Turn the filling into the pie shell.

While the filling is still hot, prepare the meringue. Beat the egg whites, vanilla, and cream of tartar until the mixture holds stiff peaks. Gradually add the sugar, 1 tablespoon at a time, beating until very stiff and glossy. All the sugar must be dissolved. Spread the meringue over the hot filling, sealing it to the edge of the crust. Bake 12 to 15 minutes or until golden brown. Cool, and chill for 2 hours before serving.

NO. 291

EASY CHOCOLATE COCONUT MERINGUE PIE

One 9-inch single-crust pie

Follow the recipe for Easy Coconut Cream Meringue Pie (No. 290), substituting chocolate pudding mix for coconut pudding mix.

No. 292   **EASY MOCHA ALMOND PIE**
One 9-inch single-crust pie

Prebaked 9-inch pie shell
(Graham Cracker Crust)
  1 **package (3½ ounces)**   ⅓ **cup sour cream**
     chocolate pudding mix   ½ **cup toasted slivered**
  2 **cups milk**   **almonds**
  1 **tablespoon instant coffee**
     powder

Prepare the prebaked pie shell; cool completely.

Combine the pudding mix, milk, and coffee powder in a saucepan. Bring the mixture to a full boil, stirring constantly. Remove the pan from the heat. Cool for 5 minutes. Mix in the sour cream and almonds. Turn the filling into the pie shell. Chill until set, at least 2 hours.

No. 293   **EASY VANILLA ALMOND PIE**
One 9-inch single-crust pie

Follow the recipe for Easy Mocha Almond Pie (No. 292), substituting vanilla pudding mix for chocolate pudding mix and omitting the coffee powder.

No. 294   **EASY LEMON PIE**
One 9-inch single-crust pie

Prebaked 9-inch pie shell
(Classic Single Crust or Graham Cracker Crust)
  1 **package (3½ ounces)**   1 **teaspoon grated lemon**
     lemon pudding mix   **zest**
  2 **cups milk**   ¼ **teaspoon ground nutmeg**
  2 **egg yolks, beaten**

Prepare the prebaked pie shell; cool completely.

Combine the pudding mix, milk, egg yolks, lemon zest, and nutmeg in a saucepan. Bring the mixture to a full boil, stirring constantly. Remove the pan from the heat. Cool for 5 minutes. Turn the filling into the pie shell. Chill until set, at least 2 hours.

NO. 295　　　　　**EASY LEMON MERINGUE PIE**

One 9-inch single-crust pie

Recipe for Easy Lemon Pie (No. 294)

Meringue

3 large egg whites, at room temperature	¼ teaspoon cream of tartar
½ teaspoon vanilla extract	6 tablespoons superfine sugar

Prepare the recipe for Easy Lemon Pie. Preheat the oven to 350° F.

While the filling is still hot, prepare the meringue. Beat the egg whites, vanilla, and cream of tartar until the mixture holds stiff peaks. Gradually add the sugar, 1 tablespoon at a time, beating until very stiff and glossy. All the sugar must be dissolved. Spread the meringue over the hot filling, sealing it to the edge of the crust. Bake 12 to 15 minutes or until golden brown. Chill before serving, at least 2 hours.

NO. 296　　　　**EASY PEACH PECAN CUSTARD PIE**

One 9-inch single-crust pie

Prebaked 9-inch pie shell
(Graham Cracker Crust)

1 package (3½ ounces) egg custard mix	¼ cup pecans, coarsely chopped
2 cups milk	1½ cups peeled, sliced peaches
¼ teaspoon nutmeg	

Prepare the prebaked pie shell; cool completely.

Combine the custard mix and milk in a saucepan. Bring the mixture to a full boil, stirring constantly. Remove the pan from the heat. Cool for 5 minutes. Mix in the nutmeg, pecans, and ½ cup of the peaches. Turn the filling into the pie shell. Chill until set, for at least 2 hours.

Arrange the remaining peaches on top of the pie before serving.

NO. 297   **EASY PISTACHIO CREAM PIE**
                                    One 9-inch single-crust pie

Prebaked 9-inch pie shell
(Graham Cracker Crust)
  1 package (3½ ounces)   1 cup sweetened whipped
    pistachio pudding mix   cream
  2 cups milk   ¼ cup unsalted (shelled)
                                             pistachio nuts

Prepare the prebaked pie shell; cool completely.

Combine the pudding mix and milk in a saucepan. Bring the mixture to a full boil, stirring constantly. Remove the pan from the heat. Cool for 5 minutes. Fold in the whipped cream. Turn the filling into the pie shell. Sprinkle with pistachio nuts. Chill until set, at least 2 hours.

NO. 298   **EASY RASPBERRY MOUSSE PIE**
                                    One 9-inch single-crust pie

Prebaked 9-inch pie shell
(Graham Cracker Crust)
  1 package (3½ ounces)   ⅓ cup sour cream
    instant raspberry mousse   1 cup fresh raspberries
    mix
  1 cup milk

Prepare the prebaked pie shell; cool completely.

Beat the mousse mix with the milk until thick, about 3 minutes. Mix in the sour cream. Turn the filling into the pie shell. Chill until set, at least 2 hours. Arrange the raspberries on top of the pie just before serving.

NO. 299   **EASY STRAWBERRY MOUSSE PIE**
                                    One 9-inch single-crust pie

Follow the recipe for Easy Raspberry Mousse Pie (No. 298), substituting strawberry mousse mix for raspberry mousse mix and fresh, sliced strawberries for raspberries.

NO. 300 **EASY STRAWBERRY SHORTCAKE PIE**

One 9-inch single-crust pie

Prebaked 9-inch pie shell
(Graham Cracker Crust)
1 package (3½ ounces)
   custard pudding mix
2 cups milk
1 cup sweetened whipped
   cream

4 ¾-inch-thick slices pound
   cake, crumbled
2 cups fresh sliced
   strawberries

Prepare the prebaked pie shell; cool completely.

Combine the pudding mix and milk in a saucepan. Bring the mixture to a full boil, stirring constantly. Remove the pan from the heat. Cool for 5 minutes. Fold in the whipped cream. Add the pound cake and one cup of the strawberries. Turn the filling into the pie shell. Chill until set, at least 2 hours. Arrange the remaining strawberries on top of the pie just before serving.

NO. 301 **EASY BANANA TRIFLE PIE**

One 9-inch single-crust pie

Follow the recipe for Easy Strawberry Shortcake Pie (No. 300), substituting 2 cups of sliced bananas for the strawberries.

NO. 302 **EASY MIXED FRUIT TRIFLE PIE**

One 9-inch single-crust pie

Follow the recipe for Easy Strawberry Shortcake Pie (No. 300), substituting 2 cups of prepared mixed fresh fruit for the strawberries.

Tarts

A homemade tart is always elegant and often extraordinary. Well-made tart pans of all sizes should always have a removable bottom. Just before serving, slip the "ring" off the crust. A small bowl placed underneath the tart makes it simple to slide the tart directly onto an attractive serving plate. Individual, petite tartlets are delicious—just reduce the baking time proportionally to the size of the pan(s) used. Many of the tarts in this chapter use a jam and liqueur glaze for extra flavor.

ALMOND TART

One 9-inch tart

Pastry for a 9-inch tart shell
(Sweet Crust)
- ½ cup unsalted butter or
  margarine, softened
- ⅔ cup sugar
- 1⅓ cups ground almonds
- 3 eggs

- 1 tablespoon rum
- ¼ teaspoon almond extract
- 1 cup slivered blanched
  almonds

Glaze

¼ cup apricot jam   2 tablespoons rum

Preheat the oven to 400° F. Prepare the pastry. Line the tart pan with the dough. Trim and crimp the edges.

Cream the butter. Mix together the sugar and ground almonds. Add one third of the sugar mixture to the butter. Beat in one egg. Stir in another third of the sugar mixture. Beat in the second egg. Add the final third of the sugar mixture. Beat in the third egg. Stir in the rum and almond extract. Turn the filling into the crust. Sprinkle with blanched almonds.

Bake 35 minutes. While the tart is still hot, prepare the glaze. In a saucepan set over very low heat, melt the jam with the rum, stirring constantly. Brush over the tart to glaze.

NO. 304   **APPLE TART I**

One 9-inch tart

Pastry for a 9-inch tart shell
(Sweet Crust)

8 medium-size tart apples   2 tablespoons grated lemon
⅓ cup sugar   zest
¼ cup plus 2 tablespoons   ¼ cup ground almonds
  unsalted butter or   2 tablespoons apricot jam
  margarine   1 tablespoon honey

Glaze

¼ cup apricot jam   2 tablespoons rum

Preheat the oven to 350° F. Prepare the pastry. Line the tart pan
with the dough. Trim and crimp the edges.

Peel, core, and dice 5 of the apples. Mix the apples with the
sugar. Melt ¼ cup of the butter, and sauté the apple mixture.
Cook stirring frequently, for 5 to 7 minutes until the apples are
golden brown. Remove the pan from the heat. Stir in the lemon
zest, almonds, and jam. Cool, and turn the filling into the crust.
Peel, core, and thinly slice the remaining apples. Arrange the apple
slices in overlapping rings on top of the filling. Melt the remaining
butter with the honey and drizzle over the apples.

Bake 35 to 40 minutes or until the pastry is golden brown.
While the tart is still hot, prepare the glaze. In a saucepan set
over very low heat, melt the jam with the rum, stirring constantly.
Brush the glaze over the tart.

NO. 305   **APPLE PRUNE TART**

One 9-inch tart

Follow the recipe for Apple Tart I (No. 304), substituting for the
sliced apples 1 cup of quartered, pitted prunes soaked in ½ cup
of rum. Bake as directed.

NO. 306   **APPLE TART II**
One 9-inch tart

Pastry for a 9-inch tart shell
(Sweet Crust)
8 Golden Delicious apples   1 teaspoon grated lemon
¼ cup unsalted butter or   zest
   margarine   ¼ cup confectioners' sugar

Glaze

½ cup orange marmalade   ¼ cup toasted, blanched
2 tablespoons water   almonds, coarsely
2 tablespoons Grand   chopped
   Marnier liqueur

Preheat the oven to 400° F. Prepare the pastry. Line the tart pan
with the dough. Trim and crimp the edges.

Peel, core, and thinly slice 5 of the apples. Melt the butter, and
sauté the apples. Cook stirring frequently, for 5 to 7 minutes, until
the apples are golden brown. Remove the pan from the heat. Stir
in the lemon zest. Cool. Turn the filling into the crust. Peel, core,
and thinly slice the remaining apples. Arrange the apple slices in
overlapping rings on top of the filling. Sprinkle confectioners' sugar
evenly over the apples.

Bake 35 to 40 minutes or until the pastry is golden brown.
While the tart is still hot, prepare the glaze. In a saucepan set
over very low heat, combine the marmalade, water, and Grand
Marnier. Cook, stirring constantly, until liquid. Brush the glaze
over the tart and sprinkle with almonds.

NO. 307   **BANBURY TART**

One 9-inch tart

Pastry for a 9-inch tart shell
(Sweet Crust)

1 cup sugar   2 tablespoons lemon juice
2 tablespoons bread crumbs   2 tablespoons grated lemon
¼ cup walnuts, coarsely   zest
   chopped   2 tablespoons unsalted
1 cup raisins, coarsely   butter or margarine
   chopped   Sweetened whipped cream
1 egg, beaten

Preheat the oven to 400° F. Prepare the pastry. Line the tart pan
with the dough. Trim and crimp the edges.

In the top of a double boiler set over simmering water, combine
the sugar, bread crumbs, walnuts, raisins, egg, lemon juice, lemon
zest, and butter. Cook, stirring frequently, until thickened. Remove
the pan from the heat. Turn the filling into the crust.

Bake 15 to 18 minutes or until golden brown. Serve with sweetened whipped cream.

NO. 308   **CHERRY TART**

One 9-inch tart

Prebaked 9-inch tart shell
(Sweet Crust)

¼ cup light brown sugar,   1 tablespoon grated lemon
   firmly packed   zest
1 cup cherry juice   4 cups halved, pitted fresh
2 tablespoons cornstarch   sweet cherries
2 tablespoons lemon juice   ¼ cup hazelnuts, coarsely
                                        chopped
                                     Vanilla ice cream

Prepare the prebaked tart shell; cool completely.

In a saucepan, combine the sugar, cherry juice, cornstarch, lemon
juice, and lemon zest. Cook over medium heat, stirring constantly,
until thickened. Remove the pan from the heat. Arrange the cherries in the bottom of the tart shell. Pour the sugar mixture over
the cherries. Sprinkle with hazelnuts. Chill until set. Serve with
vanilla ice cream.

NO. 309

COCONUT TART
One 9-inch tart

Pastry for a 9-inch tart shell
(Sweet Crust)

  6 eggs
¾ cup dark brown sugar,
    firmly packed
½ cup rum
  1 teaspoon grated lemon
    zest

¼ teaspoon nutmeg
¼ teaspoon cinnamon
1½ cups packaged
    unsweetened shredded
    coconut

Preheat the oven to 375° F. Prepare the pastry. Line the tart pan with the dough. Trim and crimp the edges.

Beat the eggs until thick and foamy. Gradually beat in the sugar. Add the rum, lemon zest, nutmeg, and cinnamon. Mix in the coconut. Turn the filling into the crust.

Bake 35 to 40 minutes or until the filling is set.

NO. 310

CRANBERRY TART
One 9-inch tart

Pastry for a 9-inch tart shell
(Sweet Crust)

  2 cups cranberries
½ cup raisins
  1 tablespoon chopped citron
  1 cup water
  1 cup sugar

½ cup bread crumbs
  1 egg, beaten
  1 teaspoon grated orange
    zest
  1 tablespoon orange juice

Preheat the oven to 350° F. Prepare the pastry. Line the tart pan with the dough. Trim and crimp the edges.

In a saucepan, combine the cranberries, raisins, citron, and water. Bring to a boil and cook, stirring frequently, until the cranberries burst. Remove the pan from the heat. Stir in the sugar. Mix together the bread crumbs, egg, orange zest, and orange juice. Add the bread crumb mixture to the cranberry mixture. Mix well. Turn the filling into the crust.

Bake 35 to 40 minutes or until the pastry is golden brown.

NO. 311   **LEMON TART**

One 9-inch tart

Prebaked 9-inch tart shell
(Sweet Crust)

1½ cups water
¾ cup sugar
2 teaspoons grated lemon
   zest
2 tablespoons cornstarch
2 egg yolks, beaten
2 tablespoons unsalted
   butter or margarine

6 tablespoons lemon juice
½ cup heavy cream
4 large macaroons, crumbled
½ cup apricot jam
2 whole thin-skinned
   lemons, very thinly
   sliced

Prepare the prebaked tart shell; cool completely.

In the top of a double boiler set over simmering water, combine 1 cup of the water, the sugar, and lemon zest. Bring the mixture to a boil. Mix the cornstarch with the remaining water and add to the hot mixture. Cook, stirring frequently for 20 minutes or until thickened. Stir a small amount of the hot mixture into the egg yolks. Combine the egg yolk mixture with the mixture in the double boiler. Cook for 2 minutes more. Remove the pan from the heat. Stir in the butter. Add the lemon juice and cool. Whip the cream. Fold the cream and macaroons into the custard. Turn the filling into the tart shell.

Melt the apricot jam until liquid. Dip each lemon slice into the jam and arrange in overlapping rings on top of the filling. Chill before serving.

NO. 312   **ORANGE TART**

One 9-inch tart

Follow the recipe for Lemon Tart (No. 311), substituting orange juice, orange zest, and oranges for the lemon juice, lemon zest, and lemons. Reduce the quantity of sugar to ½ cup.

NO. 313   **PECAN TART**

One 9-inch tart

Pastry for a 9-inch tart shell (Sweet Crust)

- ⅔ cup dark brown sugar, firmly packed
- ¼ cup heavy cream
- ¼ cup honey
- 2 tablespoons unsalted butter or margarine, melted
- 2 eggs, beaten
- ½ cup packaged unsweetened shredded coconut
- ⅔ cup pecans, coarsely chopped
- Sweetened whipped cream

Preheat the oven to 350° F. Prepare the pastry. Line the tart pan with the dough. Trim and crimp the edges.

Mix together the sugar, cream, honey, butter, eggs, coconut, and pecans. Turn the filling into the crust.

Bake 30 to 35 minutes or until pastry is golden brown. Cool, and serve with sweetened whipped cream.

NO. 314   **MACADAMIA NUT TART**

One 9-inch tart

Follow the recipe for Pecan Tart (No. 313), substituting macadamia nuts for pecans. Bake as directed.

NO. 315   **WALNUT TART**

One 9-inch tart

Follow the recipe for Pecan Tart (No. 313), substituting walnuts for pecans. Bake as directed.

NO. 316   **WALNUT FUDGE TART**

One 9-inch tart

Follow the recipe for Pecan Tart (No. 313), substituting walnuts for pecans and adding ½ cup of semi-sweet chocolate morsels to the filling. Bake as directed.

NO. 317   **PLUM TART**
                                          One 9-inch tart

Prebaked 9-inch tart shell
(Graham Cracker Crust)
  4 cups peeled, sliced plums   ¼ cup hazelnuts, coarsely
  ¾ cup apricot jam   chopped
  2 tablespoons brandy   2 tablespoons unsalted
                                            butter or margarine

Preheat the oven to 375° F. Prepare the prebaked tart shell; cool completely.

Arrange the plums in concentric circles over the bottom of the tart shell. In a saucepan set over very low heat, melt the jam with the brandy, stirring constantly. Drizzle the jam mixture over the plums. Sprinkle with the hazelnuts.

Bake 20 to 25 minutes. Serve lukewarm. (Note: this tart does not refrigerate well.)

NO. 318   **BLUEBERRY CHERRY TART**
                                          One 9-inch tart

Follow the recipe for Plum Tart (No. 317), substituting 2 cups of blueberries and 2 cups of halved, pitted sweet cherries for the plums. Bake as directed.

NO. 319   **KIWI TART**
                                          One 9-inch tart

Follow the recipe for Plum Tart (No. 317), substituting peeled, sliced kiwis for plums and raspberry jam for apricot jam. Bake as directed.

NO. 320   **PEAR TART**
                                          One 9-inch tart

Follow the recipe for Plum Tart (No. 317), substituting peeled, sliced, and cored Bosc pears for plums. Bake as directed.

NO. 321   **STRAWBERRY TART**
One 9-inch tart

Follow the recipe for Plum Tart (No. 317), substituting fresh, sliced strawberries for plums. Bake as directed.

NO. 322   **PLUM CREAM TART**
One 9-inch tart

Pastry for a 9-inch tart shell (Lemon Crust)

4 cups peeled, sliced plums	2 eggs
½ cup sugar	1 cup heavy cream
1 tablespoon cornstarch	¼ teaspoon nutmeg
1 tablespoon grated lemon zest	¼ teaspoon allspice
1 tablespoon lemon juice	

Preheat the oven to 400° F. Prepare the tart pastry. Line the tart pan with the dough. Trim and crimp the edges.

Combine the plums, sugar, cornstarch, lemon zest, and lemon juice. Mix well. Arrange the plums in concentric circles over the crust. Bake 20 minutes. Remove the tart from the oven and leave the oven on.

Beat the eggs until light and foamy. Beat in the cream, nutmeg, and allspice. Pour the egg mixture over the hot fruit and return to the oven. Bake 20 minutes more or until golden brown.

NO. 323   **NECTARINE CREAM TART**
One 9-inch tart

Follow the recipe for Plum Cream Tart (No. 322), substituting peeled, sliced nectarines for plums. Bake as directed.

NO. 324   **STRAWBERRY CUSTARD TART**

One 9-inch tart

Prebaked 9-inch tart shell
(Sweet Crust)
1½ cups milk, scalded
 ½ cup sugar
 6 tablespoons flour
 2 egg yolks, beaten
 1 teaspoon vanilla extract

2 tablespoons grated orange
   zest
¼ cup ground almonds
1½ cups sliced fresh
   strawberries

Glaze

½ cup apricot jam   2 tablespoons rum

Prepare the prebaked tart shell; cool completely.

In the top of a double boiler set over simmering water, combine ½ cup of the hot milk with the sugar and flour. Stir the remaining milk into the sugar mixture. Cook, stirring frequently, for 20 minutes or until thickened. Stir a small amount of the hot custard into the egg yolks. Combine the egg yolk mixture with the mixture in the double boiler. Cook for 2 minutes more. Remove the pan from the heat. Add the vanilla, orange zest, and almonds. Turn the filling into the tart shell. Arrange the strawberries on top of the filling.

Prepare the glaze. In a saucepan set over very low heat, cook the jam with the rum, stirring constantly, until liquid. Brush the tart with the glaze. Chill until ready to serve.

NO. 325   **BLUEBERRY CUSTARD TART**

One 9-inch tart

Follow the recipe for Strawberry Custard Tart (No. 324), substituting blueberries for strawberries.

NO. 326   **MIXED FRUIT CUSTARD TART**

One 9-inch tart

Follow the recipe for Strawberry Custard Tart (No. 324), substituting 1½ cups of prepared mixed fresh fruits for strawberries.

Sugar-Free Pies

These sugar-free pies will satisfy that desire for a delicious, naturally sweetened dessert. Sweet fresh fruit, nuts, lemon zest, and extra spices in an unsweetened crust are the only secret ingredients. Apple, blueberry, and cherry pies are among the enticing recipes that follow, and, as with all fruit pies, the luscious combinations possible are limited only by imagination and available ingredients.

NO. 327　　　　　　　　　**SUGAR-FREE APPLE PIE**

One 9-inch double-crust pie

Pastry for a 9-inch double-crust pie
(Classic Double Crust)

5 cups peeled, cored, and sliced sweet apples	1 teaspoon grated lemon zest
1 teaspoon cinnamon	½ cup walnuts, coarsely chopped
1 teaspoon allspice	
¼ teaspoon nutmeg	2 tablespoons unsalted butter or margarine
1 tablespoon lemon juice	

Preheat the oven to 450° F. Prepare the pie pastry. Line the pie pan with the bottom crust, using half of the dough. Keep the remaining dough chilled.

Combine the apples, cinnamon, allspice, nutmeg, lemon juice, lemon zest, and walnuts. Mix well. Turn the filling into the crust and dot with butter. Roll out the top crust and lay it on the filling. Trim off any excess dough, crimp the edges, and prick with the tines of a fork to vent.

Bake at 450° F for 10 minutes. Reduce the heat to 350° F and bake 45 minutes more or until golden brown.

NO. 328　　　　**SUGAR-FREE APPLE CHERRY PIE**

One 9-inch double-crust pie

Follow the recipe for Sugar-Free Apple Pie (No. 327), substituting 2 cups of halved, pitted fresh sweet cherries for 2 cups of the apples. Bake as directed.

NO. 329　　　　**SUGAR-FREE APPLE PEACH PIE**

One 9-inch double-crust pie

Follow the recipe for Sugar-Free Apple Pie (No. 327), substituting 2 cups of peeled, sliced peaches for 2 cups of the apples. Bake as directed.

NO. 330   **SUGAR-FREE APPLE PEAR PIE**
                        One 9-inch double-crust pie

Follow the recipe for Sugar-Free Apple Pie (No. 327), substituting
2 cups of peeled, cored, and sliced Bartlett pears for 2 cups of
the apples. Bake as directed.

NO. 331   **SUGAR-FREE APRICOT PIE**
                          One 9-inch double-crust pie

Pastry for a 9-inch double-crust pie
(Classic Double Crust)

5 cups peeled, sliced apricots	1 tablespoon orange juice
1 teaspoon cinnamon	½ cup blanched almonds, coarsely chopped
¼ teaspoon nutmeg	2 tablespoons unsalted butter or margarine
1 teaspoon grated orange zest	

Preheat the oven to 450° F. Prepare the pie pastry. Line the pie
pan with the bottom crust, using half of the dough. Keep the
remaining dough chilled.

Combine the apricots, cinnamon, nutmeg, orange zest, orange
juice, and almonds. Mix well. Turn the filling into the crust and
dot with butter. Roll out the top crust and lay it on the filling.
Trim off any excess dough, crimp the edges, and prick with the
tines of a fork to vent.

Bake at 450° F for 10 minutes. Reduce the heat to 350° F and
bake 45 minutes more or until golden brown.

NO. 332   **SUGAR-FREE APRICOT PEAR PIE**
                          One 9-inch double-crust pie

Follow the recipe for Sugar-Free Apricot Pie (No. 331), substituting
2 cups of peeled, cored, and sliced Bartlett pears for 2 cups of
the apricots. Bake as directed.

NO. 333   **SUGAR-FREE BLUEBERRY PIE**

One 9-inch double-crust pie

**Pastry for a 9-inch double-crust pie
(Classic Double Crust)**

  5 cups blueberries
  1 teaspoon cinnamon
  1 teaspoon allspice
  2 tablespoons flour
  2 teaspoons grated lemon
     zest

  1 tablespoon lemon juice
  ½ cup walnuts, coarsely
     chopped
  2 tablespoons unsalted
     butter or margarine

Preheat the oven to 450° F. Prepare the pie pastry. Line the pie pan with the bottom crust, using half of the dough. Keep the remaining dough chilled.

Combine the blueberries with the cinnamon, allspice, flour, lemon zest, lemon juice, and walnuts. Mix well. Turn the filling into the crust and dot with butter. Roll out the top crust and lay it on the filling. Trim off any excess dough, crimp the edges, and prick with the tines of a fork to vent.

Bake at 450° F for 10 minutes. Reduce the heat to 350° F and for 45 minutes more or until golden brown.

NO. 334   **SUGAR-FREE BLUEBERRY CHERRY PIE**

One 9-inch double-crust pie

Follow the recipe for Sugar-Free Blueberry Pie (No. 333), substituting 2 cups of halved, pitted fresh sweet cherries for 2 cups of blueberries. Bake as directed.

NO. 335   **SUGAR-FREE BLUEBERRY STRAWBERRY PIE**

One 9-inch double-crust pie

Follow the recipe for Sugar-Free Blueberry Pie (No. 333), substituting 2 cups of sliced strawberries for 2 cups of blueberries. Bake as directed.

NO. 336   **SUGAR-FREE CHERRY PIE**
                              One 9-inch double-crust pie

Pastry for a 9-inch double-crust pie
(Classic Double Crust)

5 cups halved, pitted fresh   1 tablespoon lemon juice
   sweet cherries   ½ cup pecans, coarsely
1 teaspoon allspice   chopped
1 teaspoon mace   2 tablespoons unsalted
3 tablespoons flour   butter or margarine
2 teaspoons grated lemon
   zest

Preheat the oven to 450° F. Prepare the pie pastry. Line the pie
pan with the bottom crust, using half of the dough. Keep the
remaining dough chilled.

Combine the cherries, allspice, mace, flour, lemon zest, lemon
juice, and pecans. Mix well. Turn the filling into the crust and dot
with butter. Roll out the top crust and lay it on the filling. Trim
off any excess dough, crimp the edges, and prick with the tines
of a fork to vent.

Bake at 450° F for 10 minutes. Reduce the heat to 350° F and
bake 45 minutes more or until golden brown.

NO. 337   **SUGAR-FREE PEACH PIE**
                              One 9-inch double-crust pie

Pastry for a 9-inch double-crust pie
(Classic Double Crust)

5 cups peeled, sliced   1 tablespoon lemon juice
   peaches   ½ cup walnuts, coarsely
2 teaspoons cinnamon   chopped
½ teaspoon nutmeg   2 tablespoons unsalted
                                        butter or margarine

Preheat the oven to 450° F. Prepare the pie pastry. Line the pie
pan with the bottom crust, using half of the dough. Keep the
remaining dough chilled.

Combine the peaches, cinnamon, nutmeg, lemon juice, and walnuts. Mix well. Turn the filling into the crust and dot with butter.
Roll out the top crust and lay it on the filling. Trim off any excess

dough, crimp the edges, and prick with the tines of a fork to vent.

Bake at 450° F for 10 minutes. Reduce the heat to 350° F and bake 45 minutes more or until golden brown.

NO. 338   ## SUGAR-FREE NECTARINE PIE
One 9-inch double-crust pie

Follow the recipe for Sugar-Free Peach Pie (No. 337), substituting peeled, sliced nectarines for peaches. Bake as directed.

NO. 339   ## SUGAR-FREE PEAR PIE
One 9-inch double-crust pie

Follow the recipe for Sugar-Free Peach Pie (No. 337), substituting peeled, cored, and sliced Bartlett pears for peaches. Bake as directed.

NO. 340   ## SUGAR-FREE STRAWBERRY PIE
One 9-inch lattice-top pie

Pastry for a 9-inch lattice-top pie
(Classic Double Crust)

4 cups sliced fresh strawberries	1 tablespoon lemon juice
1 teaspoon cinnamon	½ cup hazelnuts, coarsely chopped
1 teaspoon allspice	2 tablespoons unsalted butter or margarine
1 teaspoon lemon zest	1 egg yolk, beaten

Preheat the oven to 450° F. Prepare the pie pastry. Line the pie pan with the bottom crust, using half of the dough. Keep the remaining dough chilled.

Combine the strawberries, cinnamon, allspice, lemon zest, and lemon juice. Mix well. Turn the filling into the crust. Sprinkle the hazelnuts on top and dot with butter. Lay on the lattice strips and crimp the pie. Brush the lattice strips with egg yolk.

Bake at 450° F for 10 minutes. Reduce the heat to 350° F and bake 35 to 40 minutes more or until golden brown.

Savory Pies and Quiches

No pie cookbook would be complete without a chapter on main course pies. Served with a simple mixed salad and a loaf of fresh bread, these savory pies and quiches each make an appetizing one-dish meal. From old-fashioned chicken pot pie and shepherd's pie to onion pie and a broccoli cheese quiche, here are an assortment of country-style and international favorites. Also included are recipes for using up cooked meat or poultry in a selection of pot pies that puts the flavor back into leftovers.

BEEF PIE

One 9-inch double-crust pie

 2 tablespoons olive oil
 3 cloves garlic, crushed
 1 medium-size onion, peeled
    and thinly sliced
1½ pounds stewing beef,
    cubed
 3 tablespoons flour
 1 cup tomato juice
 1 cup dry white wine
 1 stalk celery, diced
 2 carrots, peeled and cut
    into ½-inch strips
10 whole button mushrooms

1 teaspoon whole caraway
   seed
½ teaspoon hot paprika
¼ teaspoon cinnamon
2 bay leaves
1 teaspoon herbes de
   Provence
1 teaspoon salt
1 teaspoon freshly grated
   black pepper
  Pastry for a 9-inch double-
   crust pie
  (Classic Double Crust)
2 tablespoons milk

Heat the olive oil in a Dutch oven. Add the garlic and onion and sauté briefly. Dredge the beef in the flour. Add to the Dutch oven and brown, stirring constantly. Add the tomato juice, wine, celery, carrots, mushrooms, caraway seed, paprika, cinnamon, bay leaves, herbes de Provence, salt, and pepper. Bring to a boil. Cover and reduce the heat to low. Simmer for 1 hour, stirring occasionally. Remove the pan from the heat. Remove the bay leaves.

When the filling is prepared, preheat the oven to 500° F. Prepare the pie pastry. Line the pie pan with the bottom crust, using half of the dough. Turn the filling into the crust. Roll out the top crust and lay it on the filling. Trim off any excess dough, crimp the edges, and cut several slits in the top to vent. Brush the pie with milk.

Bake at 500° F for 15 minutes. Reduce the heat to 375° F and bake 20 minutes more or until golden brown. Serve hot.

BEEF POT PIE

One 9-inch single-crust pie

Recipe for Beef Pie (No. 341)
Pastry for a 9-inch single-crust pie
(Baking Powder Crust)

Prepare the recipe for Beef Pie. When the filling is ready, preheat the oven to 425° F. Prepare the pastry. Thoroughly butter the bottom and sides of a 9-inch deep-dish pie pan. Turn the stew into the pie pan. Roll out the dough and lay it on the crust. Trim off any excess dough, crimp the edges, and cut several slits in the top to vent.

Bake 25 to 30 minutes or until golden brown. Serve hot.

NO. 343   **CHICKEN PIE**

One 9-inch double-crust pie

1½ pounds skinned boneless chicken breasts
2 cups chicken broth
½ cup dry sherry
2 teaspoons rosemary
3 medium-size potatoes, peeled and diced
4 carrots, peeled and cut into ½-inch strips
10 button mushrooms
1 tablespoon chopped Italian parsley

1 teaspoon thyme
½ teaspoon hot paprika
1 teaspoon salt
1 teaspoon black pepper
2 tablespoons butter
1 tablespoon flour
Pastry for a 9-inch double-crust pie
(Classic Double Crust)
2 tablespoons milk

In a large saucepan, combine the chicken, broth, sherry, and rosemary. Bring to a boil. Reduce the heat to low. Cover and simmer for 10 minutes. Remove the chicken from the pan. Stir in the potatoes, carrots, mushrooms, parsley, thyme, paprika, salt, and pepper. Cook, stirring occasionally, until potatoes are tender. Remove the pan from the heat. Cut the chicken into bite-sized pieces. Strain the vegetables, reserving the liquid, and add to the chicken. Mix the butter into the hot liquid. Using a whisk, stir in the flour. Taste, and adjust seasoning as needed. Stir the chicken mixture into the sauce.

When the filling is prepared, preheat the oven to 500° F. Prepare the pie pastry. Line the pie pan with the bottom crust, using half of the dough. Turn the filling into the crust. Roll out the top crust and lay it on the filling. Trim off any excess dough, crimp the edges, and cut several slits in the top to vent. Brush the pie with milk.

Bake at 500° F for 15 minutes. Reduce the heat to 375° F and bake 20 minutes more or until golden brown. Serve hot.

NO. 344

CHICKEN POT PIE

One 9-inch single-crust pie

Recipe for Chicken Pie (No. 343)
Pastry for a 9-inch single-crust pie
(Baking Powder Crust)

Prepare the recipe for Chicken Pie. When the filling is ready, preheat the oven to 425° F. Prepare the pastry. Thoroughly butter the bottom and sides of a 9-inch deep-dish pie pan. Turn the filling into the pie pan. Roll out the dough and lay it on the crust. Trim off any excess dough, crimp the edges, and cut several slits in the top to vent.

Bake 25 to 30 minutes or until golden brown. Serve hot.

NO. 345

CHICKEN CACCIATORE PIE

One 9-inch double-crust pie

3 tablespoons olive oil
3 cloves garlic, crushed
1 medium onion, peeled and thinly sliced
2 cups thinly sliced mushrooms
1½ pounds skinned boneless chicken breasts, cubed
1 teaspoon thyme
1 teaspoon oregano
½ teaspoon rosemary
1 teaspoon salt
1 teaspoon black pepper
2 cups canned crushed tomatoes
½ teaspoon grated lemon zest
1½ cups dry white wine
Pastry for a 9-inch double-crust pie
(Classic Double Crust)
2 tablespoons milk

Heat the olive oil in a dutch oven. Sauté the garlic and onion over medium heat until the onion is golden brown. Stir in the mushrooms and chicken. Cook, stirring frequently, for 5 minutes. Add the thyme, oregano, rosemary, salt, pepper, tomatoes, lemon zest, and wine. Bring to a boil. Cover and reduce the heat to low. Simmer for 15 to 20 minutes. Taste, and adjust seasonings. Remove the pan from the heat.

When the filling is cooked, preheat the oven to 500° F. Prepare the pie pastry. Line the pie pan with the bottom crust, using half of the dough. Turn the filling into the crust. Roll out the top crust and lay it on the filling. Trim off any excess dough, crimp the edges, and cut several slits in the top to vent. Brush the pie with milk.

Bake at 500° F for 15 minutes. Reduce the heat to 375° F and bake 20 minutes more or until golden brown. Serve hot.

NO. 346   **VEAL CACCIATORE PIE**

One 9-inch double-crust pie

Follow the recipe for Chicken Cacciatore Pie (No. 345), substituting bite-sized pieces of veal scallopini for chicken. Bake as directed.

NO. 347   **LEFTOVER LAMB POT PIE**

One 9-inch single-crust pie

3 tablespoons butter
1 medium-size onion, thinly sliced
1 cup thinly sliced mushrooms
2 cups diced cooked lamb
1 cup cooked peas
1 cup sliced, cooked carrots
½ cup dry white wine
1 cup chicken broth

½ teaspoon hot paprika
1 teaspoon herbes de Provence
1 teaspoon salt
1 teaspoon freshly grated black pepper
Pastry for a 9-inch single-crust pie
(Baking Powder Crust)

In a large saucepan, melt the butter. Add the onion and mushrooms and sauté for 5 minutes, stirring frequently. Mix in the lamb, peas, carrots, wine, broth, paprika, herbes de Provence, salt, and pepper. Bring to a boil. Cover and reduce the heat to low. Simmer for 10 minutes. Remove the pan from the heat.

When the filling is ready, preheat the oven to 425° F. Prepare the pastry. Thoroughly butter the bottom and sides of a deep-dish pie pan. Turn the filling into the pie pan. Roll out the dough and lay it on the crust. Trim off any excess dough, crimp the edges, and cut several slits in the top to vent.

Bake 25 to 30 minutes or until golden brown. Serve hot.

NO. 348   **LEFTOVER BEEF POT PIE**
One 9-inch single-crust pie

Follow the recipe for Leftover Lamb Pot Pie (No. 347), substituting cooked beef for cooked lamb. Bake as directed.

NO. 349   **LEFTOVER CHICKEN POT PIE**
One 9-inch single-crust pie

Follow the recipe for Leftover Lamb Pot Pie (No. 347), substituting cooked chicken for cooked lamb. Bake as directed.

NO. 350   **LEFTOVER PORK POT PIE**
One 9-inch single-crust pie

Follow the recipe for Leftover Lamb Pot Pie (No. 347), substituting cooked pork for cooked lamb. Add 1 teaspoon of dried sage to the filling. Bake as directed.

NO. 351   **LEFTOVER TURKEY POT PIE**
One 9-inch single-crust pie

Follow the recipe for Leftover Lamb Pot Pie (No. 347), substituting cooked turkey for cooked lamb. Bake as directed.

NO. 352   **ONION PIE**
One 9-inch single-crust pie

¼ cup unsalted butter or margarine
2 cups peeled, thinly sliced onions
4 eggs, beaten
½ cup heavy cream
⅛ teaspoon nutmeg
1 teaspoon salt
2 teaspoons black pepper
½ teaspoon hot paprika
1 cup grated Swiss cheese
Pastry for a 9-inch single-crust pie
(Classic Single Crust)

In a large saucepan, melt the butter. Add the onions and sauté until golden brown. Remove the pan from the heat. Combine the onion mixture, eggs, cream, nutmeg, salt, pepper, paprika, and cheese. Mix well.

When the filling is prepared, preheat the oven to 425° F. Prepare the pie pastry. Line the pie pan with the dough. Trim and crimp the edges. Turn the filling into the crust.

Bake 20 to 25 minutes or until the pastry is golden brown and the filling is set. Serve hot.

NO. 353   **CORN PIE**
One 9-inch single-crust pie

2 cups drained canned corn
  or cooked fresh corn
¼ cup unsalted butter or
  margarine, melted
4 eggs, beaten
½ cup heavy cream
⅛ teaspoon nutmeg
1 teaspoon salt

2 teaspoons black pepper
½ teaspoon hot paprika
1 cup grated cheddar cheese
  Pastry for a 9-inch single-
  crust pie
  (Classic Single Crust)

Combine the corn, butter, eggs, cream, nutmeg, salt, pepper, paprika, and cheese. Mix well.

When the filling is prepared, preheat the oven to 425° F. Prepare the pie pastry. Line the pie pan with the dough. Trim and crimp the edges. Turn the filling into the crust.

Bake 20 to 25 minutes or until the pastry is golden brown and the filling is set. Serve hot.

NO. 354   **SPINACH PIE**
One 9-inch single-crust pie

Follow the recipe for Corn Pie (No. 353), substituting cooked chopped spinach for the corn and crumbled feta cheese for the cheddar cheese. Bake as directed.

NO. 355

POTATO PIE

One 9-inch single-crust pie

¼ cup unsalted butter or
    margarine
1 medium-size onion, thinly
    sliced
3 cups cooked sliced
    potatoes
½ cup grated Parmesan
    cheese
½ cup grated mozzarella
    cheese

2 eggs, beaten
¼ cup milk
1 teaspoon salt
2 teaspoons oregano
¼ teaspoon nutmeg
2 teaspoons black pepper
Pastry for a 9-inch single-
    crust pie
(Classic Single Crust)

Preheat the oven to 425° F. Prepare the pie pastry. Line the pie pan with the dough. Trim and crimp the edges.

In a saucepan, melt the butter and sauté the onion until golden brown. Remove the pan from the heat. Stir in the potatoes. Mix together the Parmesan and mozzarella cheeses. Combine the eggs, milk, salt, oregano, nutmeg, and pepper. Arrange the potato and cheese mixture in alternating layers in the crust. Pour the egg mixture over the top layer.

Bake 25 to 30 minutes or until the pastry is golden brown and the filling is set. Serve hot.

NO. 356

SHEPHERD'S PIE

One 9-inch single-crust pie

2 pounds ground beef
2 tablespoons unsalted
    butter or margarine
1 medium-size onion, thinly
    sliced
2 tablespoons chopped
    Italian parsley
1 cup cooked peas
1 cup sliced, cooked carrots
1 teaspoon oregano

1 teaspoon salt
2 teaspoons black pepper
3 cups mashed potatoes
Pastry for a 9-inch single-
    crust pie
(Classic Single Crust)
Paprika

In a saucepan, sauté the beef until brown. Remove the beef from the pan and drain off the fat. Melt the butter. Simmer the onion with the parsley until golden brown. Remove the pan from the heat. Stir in the cooked beef, peas, carrots, oregano, salt, pepper, and one cup of the potatoes.

When filling is prepared, preheat the oven to 500° F. Prepare the pie pastry. Line the pie pan with the dough. Trim and crimp the edges. Turn the filling into the crust. Spread the remaining potatoes on top. Sprinkle with paprika.

Bake at 500° F for 15 minutes. Reduce the heat to 375° F and bake about 35 minutes more or until golden brown. Serve hot.

NO. 357   **CHEESE QUICHE**

One 9-inch quiche

Prebaked 9-inch quiche shell
(Butter Crust)

4 strips lean bacon	½ teaspoon black pepper
4 eggs, beaten	½ teaspoon salt
1 cup heavy cream or plain yogurt	1½ cups grated Gruyère cheese
1 cup milk	¼ cup grated Parmesan cheese
⅛ teaspoon nutmeg	

Prepare the prebaked quiche shell. Then, preheat the oven to 325° F.

In a saucepan, sauté the bacon until crisp. Remove the pan from the heat. Drain, and crumble the bacon. Beat together the eggs, cream, milk, nutmeg, pepper, and salt. Stir in the Gruyère cheese and bacon. Turn the filling into the quiche shell. Sprinkle Parmesan cheese over the top.

Bake 45 minutes or until the filling is set. Serve warm.

NO. 358   **BROCCOLI CHEESE QUICHE**

One 9-inch quiche

Follow the recipe for Cheese Quiche (No. 357), substituting 1 cup of chopped cooked broccoli for the bacon. Bake as directed.

NO. 359 ## ZUCCHINI CHEESE QUICHE
One 9-inch quiche

Follow the recipe for Cheese Quiche (No. 357), substituting 1 cup of chopped cooked zucchini for the bacon. Bake as directed.

NO. 360 ## LEEK QUICHE
One 9-inch quiche

Prebaked 9-inch quiche shell
(Butter Crust)

¼ cup unsalted butter or margarine
3 large leeks, finely diced
4 eggs, beaten
1 cup heavy cream or plain yogurt
1 cup milk

⅛ teaspoon nutmeg
½ teaspoon salt
½ teaspoon black pepper
¼ cup grated Parmesan cheese

Prepare the prebaked quiche shell. Then, preheat the oven to 325° F.

Melt the butter in a saucepan. Sauté the leeks over medium heat for 5 minutes, stirring frequently. Beat together the eggs, cream, milk, nutmeg, salt, and pepper. Mix in the leeks. Turn the filling into the quiche shell. Sprinkle Parmesan cheese on top.

Bake 45 minutes or until the filling is set. Serve warm.

NO. 361 ## MUSHROOM QUICHE
One 9-inch quiche

Follow the recipe for Leek Quiche (No. 360), substituting 2 cups of sautéed sliced mushrooms for the leeks. Bake as directed.

NO. 362

PARSLEY QUICHE

One 9-inch quiche

Prebaked 9-inch quiche shell
(Butter Crust)

¼ cup unsalted butter or margarine
1 medium-size onion, finely diced
¼ cup chopped Italian parsley
1 tablespoon chopped chives
1 tablespoon chopped watercress
1 clove garlic, crushed

1 teaspoon grated lemon zest
½ teaspoon salt
½ teaspoon black pepper
4 eggs, beaten
1 cup heavy cream or plain yogurt
1 cup milk
¼ cup grated Parmesan cheese

Prepare the prebaked quiche shell. Then, preheat the oven to 325° F.

Melt the butter in a saucepan. Sauté the onion over medium heat for 5 minutes, stirring frequently. Stir in the parsley, chives, watercress, garlic, lemon zest, salt, and pepper. Remove the pan from the heat. Beat together the eggs, cream, and milk. Add the onion. Turn the filling into the quiche shell. Sprinkle Parmesan cheese on top.

Bake 45 minutes or until the filling is set. Serve warm.

NO. 363

TOMATO QUICHE

One 9-inch quiche

Prebaked 9-inch quiche shell (Butter Crust)

¼ cup unsalted butter or margarine

1 medium-size onion, finely diced

1 tablespoon chopped Italian parsley

1½ cups canned crushed tomatoes, drained

1 teaspoon oregano

½ teaspoon salt

½ teaspoon black pepper

4 eggs, beaten

1 cup heavy cream or plain yogurt

1 cup milk

¼ cup grated Parmesan cheese

Prepare the prebaked quiche shell. Then, preheat the oven to 325° F.

Melt the butter in a saucepan. Sauté the onion and parsley over low heat for 5 minutes, stirring frequently. Stir in the tomatoes, oregano, salt, and pepper. Remove the pan from the heat. Beat together the eggs, cream, and milk. Add the onion mixture. Turn the filling into the quiche shell. Sprinkle Parmesan cheese on top.

Bake 45 minutes or until filling is set. Serve warm.

NO. 364

SHRIMP QUICHE

One 9-inch quiche

Prebaked 9-inch quiche shell (Butter Crust)

2 cups shelled cooked shrimp, diced

1 tablespoon chopped fresh dill

½ teaspoon salt

½ teaspoon black pepper

4 eggs, beaten

1 cup heavy cream or plain yogurt

1 cup milk

¼ cup grated Parmesan cheese

Prepare the prebaked quiche shell. Then, preheat the oven to 325° F.

Combine the shrimp, dill, salt, pepper, eggs, cream, and milk. Turn the filling into the quiche shell. Sprinkle Parmesan cheese on top.

Bake 45 minutes or until filling is set. Serve warm.

NO. 365

CRAB QUICHE
One 9-inch quiche

Follow the recipe for Shrimp Quiche (No. 364), substituting crab for shrimp. Bake as directed.

Index